Behind the Scenes at
MANCHESTER UNITED

Other Manchester United books available from Orion:

The Official Manchester United Annual 2008
The Champions' Story
The Official Illustrated History of Manchester United
Manchester United: The Complete Record
Sir Alex
Legends of United

Acknowledgements

The authors would like to thank the following people for their invaluable help and support in putting this book together -

Sir Alex Ferguson and his players; David Gill; John Peters; Matt Peters; Diana Law; Phil Townsend; James Adams; Leanne Bartram; Paul Bistiaux; Steve Bower; Dave Bushell; Sir Bobby Charlton; Matt Cole; Nick Coppack; Tony Coton; Paddy Crerand; Luisa D'Aprano; Karl Evans; Steve Hall; Trish Hirst; Ben Houston; Jackie Kay; Alan Keegan; Val Lord; Trevor Lea; Brian McClair; Paul McGuinness; Dr Steve McNally; Marie Marron; Ian Marshall; Rene Meulensteen; Albert Morgan; Andrea Murphy; Beth Nicholls; Sameer Pabari; Mike Phelan; Matt Prockter; Carlos Queiroz; Ken Ramsden; Arthur Roberts; Valter di Salvo; Tony Sinclair; Clive Snell; Simon Stone; Tony Strudwick; Rob Swire; Andy Welsh; Martin Walker; James White; Mark Wylie

Personal Messages

STEVE BARTRAM
Firstly, thanks to Sir Alex, his staff and players for ensuring that we continually had something positive to write about. Thanks also to everyone who put up with me during the writing of this book, particularly Leanne for not slapping me each time I crawled upstairs a full two hours after saying 'I'll be up in five minutes.'

GEMMA THOMPSON
Thanks to everyone at the club. Also thanks to all my family and friends for their fantastic support, especially Mum, Dad, George and Jo who all lived through the experience!

This book is dedicated to Gar – thinking of you always.

Behind the Scenes at
MANCHESTER UNITED

Gemma Thompson & Steve Bartram

First published in hardback in Great Britain in 2007 by
Orion Books
an imprint of the Orion Publishing Group Ltd
Orion House, 5 Upper St Martin's Lane,
London WC2H 9EA
An Hachette Livre UK Company

1 3 5 7 9 10 8 6 4 2

A CIP catalogue record for this book is available
from the British Library.

ISBN: 978 0 7528 8948 1

Design by Goldust Design
Printed in Great Britain by Butler & Tanner, Frome and London

The Orion Publishing Group's policy is to use papers that are natural, renewable
and recyclable and made from wood grown in sustainable forests. The logging
and manufacturing processes are expected to conform to the environmental
regulations of the country of origin.

Every effort has been made to fulfil requirements with regard to reproducing
copyright material. The author and publisher will be glad to rectify any omis-
sions at the earliest opportunity.

www.orionbooks.co.uk

CONTENTS

FOREWORD

"**B**uongiorno," beams Sir Alex Ferguson as kit manager Albert Morgan rushes past the seated Scot along Carrington's first-floor balcony.

"Buongiorno … I went in your car, by the way," says Morgan, almost as an afterthought as he pauses at the double doors.

"My car? Why?"

"I was looking for something I thought was in there."

"Right. Was it?"

"No. Your keys are back in your pocket."

And with that, Morgan barges through the doors and deep into the bowels of United's Carrington training complex, presumably still searching for the mystery object.

Sir Alex smiles, shakes his head and resumes the answer he had been giving, completely unfazed by the interview's impromptu interlude. Little does he realise that, in that unguarded moment, he has shown exactly what this book is about: the unseen side of Manchester United.

It's a tale to which very few are truly privy. Everybody sees The Reds go about their business on a football pitch, but only a privileged handful see the true workings of the goliath institution United has evolved into. As writers for the club's official media, we are well placed to sample the unique family atmosphere cultivated throughout United, be it through interviewing the superstar players or playing staff football with Fred the Red.

This book is our attempt to shed some light on how such a behemoth lives and breathes on a daily basis. The running order of a typical day's training, the Academy's recruitment of the game's finest young talent, the hectic planning behind trophy presentations, and the answer to the eternal question: just how do ticket ballots work? It's all here alongside much, much more.

United's perpetual place on the back pages of Britain's tabloids could have made this project an extremely delicate affair. As it turned out, everybody around the club was incredibly obliging. Be it delaying Ole Gunnar Solskjaer from meeting his family, shoehorning a slot into David Gill's unfathomably hectic day, or watching from the tunnel as the players took to the field, not a soul stood in the way of this book. Such accommodation and cooperation wasn't a media façade, merely a wonderfully honest and unconscious look into life behind the scenes at Manchester United.

We hope you enjoy the book.

Steve Bartram and Gemma Thompson
MANCHESTER, JULY 2007

Strength and conditioning coach Mike Clegg oversees the players' workout.

Part 1

LIFE AT CARRINGTON

"It's the best place in the world. Everyone here is so humble, so simple and everyone always has a smile on their face because they love being here. I enjoy coming to training just because I know I'm going to have a good time." **LOUIS SAHA**

THE LAP OF LUXURY

1

I f you want to keep some of the world's finest sportsmen happy, on top of their game, and at the peak of fitness, building a cutting-edge training facility in which to ply their daily trade is an ideal start.

Opened in January 2000 to replace The Cliff – United's former training ground on the banks of the River Irwell – the Trafford Training Complex in Carrington is the result of the most meticulous research and attention to minutiae imaginable: the brainchild of years of international studies into how to obtain the very best from all United players.

"When we were at The Cliff we were looking for another site for years because the club had outgrown the place," says Sir Alex Ferguson.

The sun rises on a new day at Carrington

"It served a terrific purpose back in the days when we had around thirty-odd players, but by the time we left we had something like seventy players and we had to accommodate some of the younger players over at the indoor training centre, we actually built dressing rooms in there to help accommodate them.

"So we were looking for ages and we tried different places; Heaton Park, we tried to see if we could do it at Littleton Road but it was too small. Then a property developer offered us this site. [Former club secretary] Ken Merrett and I came down to see it and it was just what we needed – over a hundred acres – and we went ahead with it."

With the perfect plot snared, the manager and his staff set about researching exactly what facilities would befit a club of United's stature – clocking up numerous air miles in the process.

"We sent some of the staff to look round other clubs," recalls Sir Alex. "Les Kershaw [former Academy manager] went to see a training ground in Athens, I went to Bayern Munich's training ground, Brian Kidd [the Reds' former assistant manager] went to AC Milan's training ground, Eddie Cassin – who was maintenance at the time – went around two or three places. We just compiled what we thought were the best features of each training ground and then looked at what we needed and felt was important, and we've ended up with what we've got now."

The results are impressive. As striker Louis Saha understatedly puts it: "It's the best place in the world. Everyone here is so humble, so simple, and everyone always has a smile on their face because they love being here. They're very easy to live with and I enjoy coming to training just because I know I'm going to have a good time. Of course you experience things in your life which make you a bit down, but then you come into the best place in the world. It's an amazing place to come to."

Given the high standards inherent at a club of United's stature, it's of little surprise that no expense was spared in Carrington's construction. An initial £14 million outlay on the main building was followed by a further £8 million investment, two years later, in the Academy building situated opposite. And it's not difficult to see where the money has gone. State-of-the-art training and rehabilitation equipment, twelve outdoor pitches, an indoor swimming pool, plush changing facilities and a sprawling canteen are just some of the centre's features.

Opposite: Sir Alex Ferguson and Wayne Rooney at Carrington.

An aerial view of United's training complex.

"I remember The Cliff had a fantastic atmosphere and feeling about it, but of course with modern football you have to keep up with technology, so I think we had to have a facility like this," says Ole Gunnar Solskjaer, who joined United in 1996. "We've got everything here we need. From all the pitches down to the smallest detail of machinery for your hand-eye coordination, we've got it all. If there's anything new on the market our club always checks it out. Or we get samples of things to try out because everyone wants to be connected to United, so I always feel we're a step ahead all the time."

As well as being technologically equipped, Carrington is manned by a 50-strong army of full-time staff dedicated to the smooth running of the complex and the comfort of the players.

The family atmosphere within the confines of Carrington is apparent upon entering the main building, where receptionist Kath Phipps greets visitors. Kath has been with United since 1968 and has acted as a surrogate mother to a host of club legends. When David Beckham returned to Old Trafford in March 2007 for the UEFA charity match, he spent most of his day trying to track down Kath for a catch-up and the farewell he never managed amid the chaos of his departure to Real Madrid in 2003.

The unlikely photograph, of walking football conglomerate and mild-mannered Irlam receptionist arm-in-arm, takes pride of place on Kath's mantelpiece, and also captures the enduring nature of the Manchester United spirit.

There are few levels of command and delineation at Carrington. Players' Audis comfortably flank staff Nissans in the front car park, while the canteen queue is as lawless as that at any secondary school, embodying a lack of segregation which is a requisite of life under Sir Alex Ferguson's roof.

"It's always been good that way," says the manager, feet up, gazing out from the first floor balcony. "I think when you're searching for that and trying to develop that kind of atmosphere it's always the human being that does it.

"The people in the place have got to have the qualities whereby they can gel with one another and understand all the different personalities in a football club. But whether it's Kath Phipps on reception or the players or the girls in the kitchen, you've got to have the personalities to embroider a really good, close-knit unit. Everyone eats together, people wander about from office to office. Demarcation is never an issue here."

"Sir Alex wouldn't have it any other way," says site manager Clive Snell, the man entrusted with the smooth running of the complex. "Among the staff he very much likes a family feel. He wouldn't dare have a separate dining room for the players and coaches; he wants everyone to eat together so the likes of the office staff, ground staff and cleaning staff all do so. We all eat the same food in the same room, and the manager knows everyone. His name retention is amazing!"

Everything on the site falls within Snell's remit, be it the purchase of new equipment or checking on the club's nature reserve, which takes up 23 of the site's 108 acres, to managing the football club's 85 acres. Clive is a seasoned sheriff of the complex. But it wasn't always that way.

"I actually started here the day this place opened," he recalls. "The team came back from the World Club Championship in Brazil and just came in on my first day of work. All the staff that worked here came in too and were looking to me to be in charge! We've just evolved and more staff have moved here from Old Trafford, the football club side of things, so we've got over fifty permanent staff working here now."

Carrington is a far cry from The Cliff in terms of workforce and facilities, but also security. Gone are the heady days of wading through hordes of wide-eyed kids and opportunistic merchandise peddlers queuing for autographs. Given the celebrity status afforded modern footballers, United have to err on the side of caution.

Pondering the nightmarish scenario, Snell laughs: "Imagine if you did just allow people to walk in? They would be everywhere. We have supporters' groups, special needs kids and more all invited down to watch training but it's strictly by invitation only. The media is also by invitation only.

"We do have very, very good security. We have twenty-four-hour surveillance, CCTV cameras, three metre-high fencing all around the site, so it's as secure as you can make it without being Fort Knox. It's a shame in a way that we can't just allow kids to come down and watch training, because that's the kind of thing anybody would remember for the rest of their lives, but it's difficult."

Being shielded from distraction is just one of the luxuries the players have learned to appreciate through life at Carrington. Far from taking such comfort for granted, however, the players are more than aware of how fortunate they are.

"To be fair, we're like spoiled kids really," says John O'Shea. "We're very well looked after, everything's done for us and we've just got to turn up and go out training. That's why the club is run so well and why it's been so successful, everybody looks after each other."

"We take it for granted here because everyone's happy," concurs Ole Gunnar Solskjaer. "But when my mates come in they always comment that it's such a welcoming atmosphere. When Henrik Larsson first came, he immediately noticed that it was a family club. Everyone knows each other and that's a major aspect I think, that we all know we have to get on.

"As players, we all know that we can play well, but the staff help us concentrate on just doing that. They want to help us prepare for games and they work very hard in the background to do that. I've got absolutely nothing to complain about. If I ever build a club, it should be like this – if I have the money! It's expensive, but I think it's money well spent because it's such a nice place."

With the business element of the club based just under eight miles

Gary Neville and Wayne Rooney at the Christmas party at Carrington in 2006. 'We are looked after brilliantly,' comments the Reds' skipper.

Nemanja Vidic,
with Paul Scholes,
was delighted how
the players and staff
helped him settle in
at United.

away at Old Trafford, those at Carrington are free to concentrate on the staple matter of winning football matches.

"In the main, this football club revolves around serving the team," says club captain Gary Neville. "We are incredibly blessed to have such fantastic people around us, and to say our lives are simple is an under-statement – we are looked after brilliantly. Manchester United set incredibly high standards in the way that they look after their players, from the personal side to the professional side. The hotels we stay in, the food we eat, the kit we play in, everything is organised for us. It's incredible.

"We'd be lost without Barry Moorhouse, who looks after the players, and on the medical side we want for nothing. We are totally pampered and truly are the luckiest people in the world to play for this great foot-ball club. We don't only get paid for it, we get very well looked after too

– we are incredibly fortunate people. I'm so grateful to everyone and I fully respect the fact that I'm very lucky. I've never known anything else other than being at United. I know there is nothing that I could do in my life that would be better than playing for this incredible football club."

Although the Reds' Bury-born skipper has risen through the United ranks over the best part of a lifetime, the club's eclectic mix of nationalities means there are plenty of languages echoing around the Carrington corridors.

Every foreign signing is given as much help as they desire to learn English and get used to a new way of life. Serbian defender Nemanja Vidic is just one player who has benefited from the club's standard welcome after his January 2006 arrival from Spartak Moscow.

"I was very happy with everything when I first came here," he says. "I knew when I signed that I was joining the biggest club in the world, but the great thing was, nobody put me under too much pressure when I first joined. It was a big change for me – I'd moved to a new country and had to adapt to a new culture and a new style of football, as well as get to know my team-mates.

"The lifestyle in England is very different to that in both Moscow and Serbia. Of course my home is in Serbia, so when I was there all my family and friends were nearby. When I moved here I didn't know anyone. But my life is very simple in England and I like it very much. My mother, father and brother come to visit me which is great and I have more time for myself and for my family which I enjoy.

"When I moved here I had to change both my life and my game. The first couple of months were particularly hard and I didn't feel confident on the pitch. But if I had a bad game I never felt that anyone at the club looked at me differently or made me feel uncomfortable. All the players and the staff supported me and helped me to improve every day so I could eventually show what I could really do. There was always someone I could turn to which was fantastic. I've enjoyed my time here so far very much, and I love everything about playing for United."

With Vidic and his colleagues equipped, comfortable and shielded from prying eyes, it's time to set about the business of becoming the best around.

PRACTICE MAKES PERFECT

2

By 7.30 a.m. on most weekday mornings, the hood of Sir Alex Ferguson's car is already stone cold. It's nothing to do with the invariably inclement Manchester weather, of course, but all to do with the fact that the gaffer has been perched at his desk for half an hour already. And he's not alone.

After more than two decades in the job, Sir Alex leaves the planning and execution of United's training sessions to assistant manager Carlos Queiroz and first team coach Mike Phelan. They, together with goalkeeping coach Tony Coton, fitness coach Tony Strudwick and skills coach Rene Meulensteen, put the players through their paces on a daily basis while Sir Alex monitors developments.

"The training session is based on one concept which we call the integration concept," says assistant manager Queiroz. "All things are related to the preparation of the players. The technical, tactical and fitness aspects, everything together is in an integrated system. Everything we do in training is related to the game and the competition.

"The most important thing is that before training, we understand the needs of each player in each position and we know the needs of the team, so we can make the right decisions. We create and combine the right harmony between the preparation of the individual and that of the team. As an example, the tactical preparations of the team, the defensive and attacking organisation, our attacking strategy, fitness – everything is structured according to this integrated model."

The need for such amalgamation prompts daily early-morning meetings. The players arrive around 9.30 a.m., half an hour before training starts, but the coaching staff meet well in advance of every session to organise each day's bespoke training programme. The club's medical staff are also consulted to highlight players' knocks and injuries, allowing the coaches to decide whether or not there will be a full complement of players, and amend their plans accordingly.

"Everybody's work is part of our integrated system to prepare the

**Opposite:
Wayne Rooney gets
set for training.**

Carlos Queiroz discusses tactics with some of the United players.

players from an individual and collective point of view," says Carlos. "Everything the player does on the pitch has different impacts in the performance of the team. If you run and shoot then there's the technical impact, the fitness impact, an emotional and mental impact. Human beings aren't split into different areas; we work through a complex system.

"Every day we have meetings where we receive different contributions from people with responsibilities in different areas, so my job is just to create the right harmony and make the right decisions in terms of preparation – which drills to do when, how many hours of training to do on each day of the week, etc. Tony's contribution, along with Mick [Phelan] and TC [Tony Coton], I would say are the most important elements of our technical staff, because through them we build up the preparation of the players."

Fitness coach Tony Strudwick arrived at Old Trafford in August 2007 from Blackburn Rovers and he is the man who keeps the players ticking over at levels of hyper-fitness.

"The training programme for the week, otherwise known as the microcycle, is determined by the amount of games we have in a week," says Strudwick. "It's difficult to plan too far in advance because we might suddenly find ourselves involved in another match, for example, an FA Cup replay. During the season very few weeks are the same, so we therefore plan the sessions on a week-by-week basis, but we always look at the programme as a whole.

"The day after a game, often Sunday, will usually be a rest day for everyone or a recovery day for those who have played. The first three days of the following week – Monday, Tuesday and Wednesday – involve a lot of hard work on the players' part. In terms of fitness training, the squad will spend some time in the gym working on building up their strength on the Monday.

"Gym work is very important for a footballer. A player's game is a mix of technical ability, endurance and strength. It's therefore important to improve the power of each player and the gym work helps to do that. The following day they will focus on aerobic work to help increase their endurance, and on the third day they will spend time on speed work.

"After three days of hard work we then start to reduce the physical pressure and intensity on the players in order to help them start preparing themselves for the game on the Saturday. We will also look at some injury prevention methods. The day before a match the players will take part in a standard training session, which lasts no longer than an hour. We try to make everything short and sharp and to help improve the neuromuscular activity so the players are ready for the game."

"We prepare them well, and we have a good group of players," adds coach Mike Phelan. "They train out on the grass, indoors and they have individual work too, so there are three aspects to how we deal with them. It's up to us to decide how we do that, when we do that and, of course, how often we do it. If we're playing games all the time then we probably do very, very little. It's just about recovering them for the next game."

The mastermind behind the technical aspect of United's training sessions is Queiroz. The Portuguese, in his second spell at the club, is well aware of the importance of practice.

"As a result of work, time and training sessions, everything seems to run more and more smoothly during the game," says Carlos. "People could imagine something happening through magic steps, but it is of course that the players are concentrating and everybody knows his responsibilities in the team.

"Everybody knows the limits to where they can go, and knowing that creates more freedom and more initiative for the others because whenever anybody does something he knows there's a team behind him. That's why things seem more simple and easy when in fact they are doing difficult things. In football, high quality movement seems to be simple but it is exactly the complexity of those movements that is the most difficult thing in the game.

"There is no perfection in football. There are always points – not always from the individual point of view, sometimes from the collective one – that have room to improve. We can do that with smart work and if everybody's ready to accept their mistakes, the things that they're not doing right, and the areas we should improve.

"I must say that what is important is that a lot of the time during games we're enjoying the games, because the lads are fantastic and we can't ask for more during games. The attitude, concentration, discipline, fantasy, responsibilities, the team spirit are fantastic. But, of course, during the week is not time to have fun. Fun comes during the games and we enjoy the performances, but during the week there is room only to work, and specifically in the areas we believe we must improve."

The first 15 minutes of training are spent on spinning bikes. The players get the blood pumping through their legs inside the wooden-sprung training hall before filtering out on to the first team training pitch. Once outside, the first drill is usually one of the players' favourites: "boxes". The squad is split into a junior and senior group, and then two members of each group are enclosed by the rest, rather predictably in a box shape. The duo's aim is to win the ball, while the remainder must keep it from them with one-touch passing.

"I love going out and doing boxes – it's the best part about training," says Rio Ferdinand. "I think ninety per cent of the lads would agree. If Carlos changes the training session around and tells us we're not doing boxes I go bananas. I need to do a box to start the day off on a good vibe! Scholesy is probably the best at boxes. His awareness and touch is always spot on. I was shocking in my first season at the club. I felt more pressure in that box than I did walking out at Old Trafford! After the first year I got used to it and I'd say I'm all right at it now."

"Scholesy and Giggsy are probably the best at boxes," adds Darren

Fletcher. "They've been at the club for such a long time so they've got the experience of doing it every day for years – they know the ins and outs of it. When you go into their box, which is the older box, it really is a step up and the play is a lot quicker. It's a good exercise, there is a lot of mickey-taking mainly because all the lads will try and nutmeg each other. We get some great little passing routines going and we've got up to around thirty passes in the past."

Having eased the players into the session gently with their light-hearted drill of choice, Queiroz and Phelan then prefer to focus on more serious matters.

"After boxes we do a little bit of function work, focusing on possession and team shape for the build-up to the next game," says Fletcher. "Training does vary – there are different shooting and tactical exercises we do, and on certain days of the week there will be specific training drills geared towards positions. The strikers, midfielders, and defenders will split up and work on their specific positions for twenty minutes or so. The midfielders will work on threading passes through the defence. It'll be four against four. The attacking quartet will aim to get the ball through the gaps, while the other team will work on staying together as a unit. For example, if the ball goes wide, we'll all move over as one group."

The goalkeepers, meanwhile, are whisked away by Tony Coton to perform their own warm up. Plenty of handling practice plus

The players take part in "boxes", one of the most popular training exercises.

Mike Phelan and Carlos Queiroz watch over the players training with Sir Alex.

two-touch footwork prepares the custodians for joining up with their outfield cohorts for the end of the session.

"We have certain things that seem to be laid down in stone," says Phelan. "In the first part of training we like to let the players enjoy themselves, just getting the balls out, knocking them about and playing little possession games. Then we move on to the main hub of the session, whatever we want to get in them for the next game or something that didn't happen in the last game. We build up the session that way.

"Sometimes we can work the whole group as one unit, or we'll put them into specific positions and work on specific areas of their game. We may concentrate on forwards, midfield, wide players, or defenders and split that up into different groups for myself and Carlos to work with. Then we bring them back together and let them play.

"I think they always enjoy the work they have to do which is specific to their position. They like to join in the overall eight v eights, or wherever there's a collection of players and they can compete against each

Rio and Co celebrate victory in an inter-squad match.

other. But the individual work, or the groups of individuals working together is then challenging them to play in positions and do things in their positions, which they seem to enjoy because it's specific for them."

In addition to focusing on their own squad's strengths, the coaching staff also find time to factor in preparatory drills to combat upcoming opponents – although typically only a small amount.

"It depends on the game or the situation we find ourselves in," says Phelan. "A lot of the time it's mainly keeping the players alive and alert and ticking over fitness-wise. We'll probably do one session on preparation for the opponents because games come so thick and fast it's difficult to do team training on the next game."

The final drill in training is usually a small sided match of between seven- and ten-a-side, depending on how bare or crowded the treatment room is looking.

"We normally always finish training with a little match," says Fletcher. "Usually seven-a-side. Some of us will swap positions during five-a-side games – the defenders might play up front and vice versa. Rio fancies himself in the free role behind the striker, while goalkeeper Tom Heaton surprised us on one occasion when he played outfield as he went and scored a hat-trick!"

"Sometimes I play upfront when we're having a joke around during a mini-match," chips in Nemanja Vidic. "I actually started out as a right winger then I went to right-back, before I finally became a central defender. I remember playing on the left wing during one training session – Cristiano took my place in central defence! I felt good on the left wing. I didn't score but I made one great run and put in a great cross but no one was there! I wasn't quite as good as Ronaldo but I wasn't bad either."

Given the eclectic composition of United's playing squad – with origins ranging from Serbia to Seoul – it's of little surprise that language disparities can provide a sizeable hurdle. Fortunately for all, Queiroz is well-versed in several tongues while several players speak more than one language.

"Things do get lost in translation," admits Lancashire-born Phelan. "But when you've got somebody who can speak certain languages you can have a direct input through them to the players, which is very important in this game now, having that kind of rapport with players.

When I say something in English, they may think they understand it, but somewhere along the line through their language it can be twisted to sound totally different, and that becomes a problem. So it is helpful having someone like Carlos who speaks different languages."

The Portuguese tactician's background has taken him around the globe. Having had jobs in South Africa, the United Arab Emirates, America, Japan and Spain, the result is that Queiroz speaks five languages, and has a wealth of cross-cultural expertise.

"Basically we try to keep all conversations in English," he says. "But sometimes there are sensitive matters that require the mother tongue to be used. When English is not your mother language, no matter how much you try to learn the language, sometimes when you try to express feelings it's better to use your mother language because you can be more accurate.

"For instance, if a player is injured, fatigued or emotionally down, then it's better to check his feelings and thoughts in his mother language. That's why in those moments that it's good I can communicate in, say, Spanish with Carlos Tevez, French with the French boys, or Portuguese with Cristiano, Nani and Anderson. But for the routine daily conversation we always try to keep English as our official language at the club. Speaking the players' mother languages helps me a lot because I can have the close approach with them.

"When you talk about Manchester United, you're talking about the highest demands because they are a group of international players who play the game at the top, top level. That level of competition demands the top level of preparation, there's no other option. The training at United demands an understanding of the roots and backgrounds of the players.

"When you work with national teams, all the players are of the same nationality and come from the same roots and backgrounds. When you then work at United you have diverse technical cultures such as Latin concepts, a continental concept of preparation and tactics. The way they approach the game is dfferent from the English style and the roots of the English players; then you have South American players and those from African backgrounds.

"The most difficult job I found was to create the right balance, because if you come here and use the traditional concept of training in England then you lose half the team. I couldn't use the methods and concepts I usually use only with Latin players because I could lose the concentration and motivation of the English players. At the beginning it was very important, through my experience and knowledge, to know and understand where they're coming from, and create training sessions where I can keep all of them at a high level of motivation and concentration, exciting the players through the backgrounds and roots that each one brought to the training session.

"I must tell you that it wasn't easy and isn't an easy task for a coach to have so many different languages and roots and keep ninety minutes of attraction to the training sessions. That's especially true when you have to be persistent and repetitive with your ideas. I thought, and I still think, that if I didn't have the experience of working with South Americans, Asian, African and European players, then it would have been problematic to prepare the players in the right way."

Part of the coaching staff's balancing act is to keep the players on top of their game with drills and fitness work, while also affording them sufficient rest during hectic gluts of games.

"You gain experience along the way because here we usually have games coming every three or four days so it's something we know how to deal with," says Mike Phelan. "We vary it every now and again so that it doesn't get boring. Some players need a bit more work, some players don't, depending on how many games they're playing and the regularity of them. We manage that among myself, Carlos and the manager. The way we get the best out of them is by keeping them fit – that always helps!"

With fitness such a key element, each player has a bespoke training programme drawn up by Tony Strudwick. Gone are the days of extra laps around The Cliff, running until legs or lungs gave out. Ole Gunnar Solskjaer has sampled the evolution of the club's training regimes first-hand since 1996.

"I think I just caught the latter end of old-school English football when I arrived," he says. "Foreign coaches, new training methods, loads of foreign players I think changed the demands of being a top player in the Premier League. You couldn't live as a top footballer now and be going out to the pub and doing what you do. I've noticed a massive difference. Everything now is down to detail. Before, in training, you ran your socks off, but now everything is more scientific. You don't have to run that hard to get fitter.

Rene Meulensteen
demonstrates one of
the skills players can
utilise during a match.

"It's energy saving and on a matchday you do feel fitter. But you have to be because the modern day footballer is so fit, athletic, technical, quick … I think that's the way it goes with life in general – everyone's just trying to be more effective and trying to find better ways to do things. I've benefited from the training methods here, I don't think I could cope with all the long slogs now at my age!"

Predictably, the players by and large enjoy their time with the ball, far more than the time devoted to fitness drills. Strudwick is resigned to the fact that his speciality dish of jogging served with lashes of sprinting is far from popular among the squad, but has nothing but praise for their dedication to hard work.

"As you'd expect the players enjoy the ball work much more than the fitness work in training," he says. "That's normal. But our players are great professionals and they fully understand the importance of the fitness training. They know that that area can also help the technical aspect of their game. They are a great group of lads and they push me and the other coaches to work them very hard. At the end of most training sessions, many of the players will stay behind and ask to do some extra work on their own, both from a technical point of view and a fitness one."

The players are, however, prone to moments of mischief when given a chance to catch their breath. "You have to have your wits about you when Scholesy and Wazza [Rooney] are around," says Darren Fletcher. "All the balls that are dotted around the edge of the pitch will suddenly start flying past you! You can never relax during that period."

Chief offender Wayne Rooney remains committed to the pursuit of hyper-fitness, however, staying true to the old 'no pain, no gain' maxim. "You've got to do the work to get the best out of yourself in the games," he concedes. "You've got to be fit and I think now with the games getting quicker you've got to be able to run for ninety minutes. Whether it's high intensity or endurance you've got to do it, and the only way you can do that for ninety minutes is by doing it in training through the week."

Whereas a player might have possession for a few minutes during a match, they have the most intense contact with the ball during training sessions. This is the time when those lucky enough to catch a glimpse of Carrington will be privy to the players' repertoire of tricks. Predictably, one man stands out above all others as the chief entertainer.

"Ronaldo's skills are even more impressive and ridiculous in training," says Darren Fletcher. "He's always trying things out and when you're up against him you really have to be on your toes because he can make you look like a fool. He invents new tricks all the time and spends a lot of time practising and mastering them. Once he's done that he's got them in the bag to pull out whenever he needs to."

While many of his mid-match tricks and skills look totally impro-vised, the Portuguese winger spends hours practising his catalogue of party-pieces. He is just one of a lengthy list to benefit from a session with technical skills coach Rene Meulensteen.

He and other Coaches provide one-on-one or small group sessions which focus on improving the players' ball skills. Such sessions can reap spectacular dividends – with Ryan Giggs the perfect example that you're never too old to learn.

"In 2006/07 he had a magnificent season, but like everyone he's human," says Rene. "A couple, maybe three years ago, he wasn't on top, top form. He needed to rediscover himself. As you get older, you pick up knocks and injuries, but you get experience as well. He makes different decisions now than he did when he was seventeen or eighteen.

"Ryan's strength is that he's got magnificent skill from himself, with a lovely element of disguise, and another was always running with the ball and manipulating it. For some reason that disappeared from his game a little, but it's back now. Because of the injuries and age, he might not have been as explosive as he was – what then helps is having turns and moves in your locker to compensate, and he's really added that to his game. You also see a lot more Cruyff turns or stepovers which have served him well.

"The older players in the latter stages of their careers have the skills, and the good thing is that you don't have to tell them when and where to use them. They have the experience to know that, it's just whether they're comfortable with certain moves. With the young kids, we give them all the optional moves and let them practise until they get to a point where they are naturally more comfortable with one or two. With the first team players you can look at them, let them do them, and then quickly rule most of them out, get them to concentrate on specific ones they are comfortable with.

"You can be very specific then. That's the core, and what it will do is add something to the game where players look to have so much time on the ball, simply because they've found the right balance between popping the ball about nice and quickly, and suddenly using a disguised piece of skill. Disguise is nothing else than making your opponent think you're going one way, then as soon as you've committed him, going the other.

"When you have that, that's when you get teams who look like they can't be caught. It's not just skill though, personality and attitude carries the skill. That's part of the development too, and that's a bit harder with the older players. They're more calculated, that's why sometimes they get caught in two minds and you can see it when they're playing. It's not a problem, you just encourage them not to get caught up in their mind. That's because they missed the chance to develop these things earlier on in their careers."

The Dutchman also works with players who are returning from injury and are unable to join in with the group, providing special sessions which are constructed after consultation with the medical staff.

"There's not a set routine that we stick to," reveals Rene. "When a player's injured, there might be certain things the medical staff don't want them to do, such as power shooting. In general, I've always worked to generally improve their skills, which relates a lot to basic things, simple things like passing, first touch, hard or soft passing, receiving the ball.

"That's the basic package, but on top of that, that's where the real core of my work lies – in the use of turns, changing the angle of attack, running at players, going past people. That always relates to the position they play. If I work with John O'Shea, who could be at right back or in central defence, he will be exposed to different one v ones than for instance Cristiano or Louis Saha."

Recuperating players are much safer honing their skills and easing their way back into the game with Meulensteen, rather than taking part in group sessions. They may be away from the pressure of playing for points in front of TV cameras and fans, but the squad still treats training as a serious matter. Nobody will shirk a challenge, regardless of friend-ships, such is the spirited mood which underscores each session.

"It's quite competitive," chuckles Rooney. "Every day there are always tackles flying in so it's the same as a game really. We take everything seriously. We still have fun and banter in training but when it comes to it, it's as serious as anything."

Fun and banter often constitutes players swapping positions, with Rooney in particular known for his fondness of donning the goalkeeper's gloves to fend off an avalanche of shots at the end of shooting practice.

"Yeah, I do like going in goal at the end," he says. "I just put the gloves on and a few of the lads have some shots at me. It's good, it's different. I like to think I'm all right. I was gutted when Edwin [van der Sar] got injured at Spurs [in February 2007], I probably would have gone in goal if I hadn't been substituted. If it happens again and I'm on the pitch then I'm sure I'll probably go in. We've just about heard the end of it from Sheasy after he kept a clean sheet, so it's my turn next time!"

"Sheasy" is, of course, John O'Shea, who further expanded his role of utility player by replacing broken nose victim Van der Sar for the final ten minutes of United's 4-0 win at White Hart Lane. Rooney could only watch from the substitutes' bench while his impromptu stopper experience

Ronaldo demonstrates one of his many skills during a game of head tennis.

went to waste, and the big Irishman ended up in goal with precious little familiarity in between the sticks.

"I'd been in goal the odd time in training, but only for a mess around – never in a pressure situation," O'Shea laughs. "Obviously when I was younger I played Gaelic football. It's not a goalkeeper but it's still using your hands, catching and punching the ball. To be fair I was just buzzing for the first few minutes and then I realised 'oh no, I've actually got to be a goalkeeper here!' It was a bit nerve-racking but I got through it OK."

Although given no dedicated training for his surprise role of custodian, O'Shea has nothing but praise for United's coaching staff.

"They're top class because of the preparation they put into everything. Carlos is the main man probably for the training, TC looks after the keepers and behind the scenes Mick [Phelan] is watching teams we're playing, getting the detail on them and individually talking to players differently. All of them to be fair do a great job, and obviously the manager does his job too. So we're spoiled by people looking after us, but also by our coaches too in the way they go into detail for every game.

"At the start of training it's fairly calm but we know that when Carlos, Mick or the manager are talking to us we need to get down and concentrate on what we're doing. That might be the different approaches we have to games and the use of different tactics or formations we may be trying. We know we have to concentrate on that and make sure we get it right. As I say, it's mainly the same but the manager and coaches try and keep the smiles on our faces all the time. Obviously we're lucky we don't work as long in a day as the normal working man and people give you grief for it, but you can only run around for so long before you collapse!"

Although it's easy to view the coach-player relations in the same vein as teachers and pupils, both parties recognise the need to work in harmony. The aim is simple – the players want to improve, the coaches are charged with improving them.

"As coaches, certainly with the first team, we spend more time with the players than with our own families at times," says Phelan. "If we're not here working then we're on the road watching games or travelling to prepare for a game. We do literally live with these players at times. We don't take them home with us, but it's near as damn-it when you're in a hotel with them. But it's a good relationship. They understand, I think, that they need coaches to prepare them, they need all that facility to prepare them and they repay us by putting in the hard work."

The affinity between players and coaches makes for great function, and the same thing goes for the rapport among all the coaching staff. Ironically, Phelan is explaining the need for staff banter when Tony Coton strolls past, pretending to yawn and loudly droning "during the war, when I had a fringe" in reference to Phelan's bald head.

Still laughing, Phelan admits: "Banter is very important. All the coaches are working towards the same aim: they're all trying to produce football players and winning teams for the club, and entertaining football for the supporters' benefit. It's something that coaches feel a big responsibility for. We're there in the background. Everybody can see that we've got talented players, but you have to get that talent out of them. Sometimes that's hard, sometimes it's easy, but the banter between the coaches is very, very good.

"The one thing that has changed is that you've got different cultures in the system. It used to be the odd player from abroad, now there are a lot of foreign players and coaches too. It brings with it all different humour, ideas and ways of doing things. Football's international, but eventually we turn them round and mould them in our own image."

"I think it's great," concurs Coton. "I'm usually the brunt of the banter, or giving it out, but it's great. Albert, Mick, Garry Armer and everyone. I've been in football all my life, I went to an all-boys school so I've been used to having blokes around me all the time. Everybody's got to have massive amounts of character to play here at United. That's where some players have failed, young and old, because they've not had that character. If you take the mickey, you've got to be able to take it back, and within that area the first team staff give it each other.

"The gaffer's the world's worst for that kind of thing. What the public sees is not what happens. The only problem with the manager is that he can't keep a straight face, he laughs too early and I tell him that. He gives it away. We have some great fun. We work hard through the week and a Friday night before a Saturday away game is usually the only time we're all sat down together. We have a meal with the manager. He'll be chatting and telling us the same story, except this time he's added something to it from two weeks ago, so you just act surprised and he doesn't realise!"

3

I PREDICT A DIET

While Sir Alex Ferguson and his players rightly grab the headlines on the back of success on the field, the United boss and his team are the first to acknowledge the contribution to the cause by the Reds' backroom ensemble. A crucial cog in the club's wheel of success, they are the unsung heroes, the people who are always ready and willing to ensure the team's every need is taken care of and the players' preparation for matches is second to none.

An important part of that preparation revolves around the fitness and medical sides of the game. Advances in scientific technology relating to both areas have resulted in giant strides being made by clubs

The players refuel in the Carrington canteen.

like United whose adage is always to remain one step ahead of the rest. The acute level of detail that now goes into the team's conditioning and preparation for games is fundamentally aided by the Reds' dedicated video analysis team.

The club's state-of-the-art video analysis room and editing suite, situated next door to the players' lounge at Carrington, comprises a vast range of equipment which allows the coaching staff to watch games from all over the world, while computers, featuring the most advanced software available, help to collate the latest stats on each player's fitness performance during matches, as well as opposition teams.

A special archive room holds clips of games from seasons gone by, as well as individual player montages, which are available for the players themselves to review. The department is run by scouting administrator Steve Brown, ably assisted by sports analyst Simon Wells and with regular input from Carlos Queiroz, Mike Phelan, Tony Coton and Tony Strudwick, whose job it is to analyse the findings.

"Technology plays a massive part in the modern-day game and one of the most important things in helping to aid the performance and fitness of each player is the match analysis that we receive after each game," explains Tony, who is responsible for taking care of the physical condition of the squad. "I spend a lot of time examining the data because it provides me with the specifics I need to understand each player's performance. It also means, if needs be, I can adjust or modify the fitness programmes I create for individual players. I discuss the data with the manager and other members of the coaching staff, as well as the players themselves. I speak to each of them on an individual basis and explain what I think they need to work on or change within their game and also what is working well for them."

According to Tony, there are two important differences among players – the first being individual and the second positional. The former refers to a player's specific characteristics such as height, weight and body structure. The latter, as the term suggests, is linked to a player's usual location on the field. Both are features that Strudwick says are continually being monitored.

"The use of statistical data is something that has come to the fore-front of the game particularly over the last few years," he explains. "The information we receive on the players shows there are big differences in terms of their fitness and work during a game relating to position. For example, the four players at the back are primarily focused on defending, but the activity that the central defenders do during a match is completely different to that which is done by the fullbacks.

"The likes of Rio [Ferdinand] and [Nemanja] Vidic, who are central defenders, will do short, sharp sprints and then may have a breather for a minute or so, whereas the fullbacks, such as Gary [Neville] and Patrice [Evra], not only have to work hard in terms of defending, they also get involved in an offensive manner when the team are on the attack. For that reason they will do much longer and greater sprints. There are differences throughout the team – the work done by a winger will be very different to that which is done by a central defender. Thanks to the statistical data we have on these positional differences we are able to organise training programmes, both with balls and without balls, which are specific to each position. I'm continuing to do a lot of research into this area of the game because we really believe the scientific aspects of football can help with the technology of training sessions."

Aside from their pre-match duties at Carrington, members of the video analysis team are also kept busy on home matchdays and, on occasion, during away trips.

"Simon [Wells] will be editing clips and collating stats during the first half which he then puts on the portable hard drive for Carlos, Mick and me to view at half time on our laptops," explains goalkeeping coach Tony Coton. "One ultra-wide-view camera shows the players like ants, but you can see the patterns of play and individual runs much more easily than you would do normally. If something happens during the first half and we need to see it, either Mick or I, or quite often both of us, will go in and ask Simon to get us the clip and it can be on our screens within seconds. It allows us to see if a player isn't tucking in, or perhaps he's getting caught up field too often, or he's not getting close enough to the opposition to stop crosses coming in. We then mention it to Carlos and he'll go and have a quiet word with the individual in question if it's an individual thing. If it's a collective thing then he can tell everyone, but quite often it's a case of having a quiet word with a player.

"After home games, Simon has the full match edited for us within an

Ji-sung Park works up
a sweat in the gym.

hour or so of the final whistle. We'll take it away and watch it at home. From a goalkeeping point of view, I won't pull the keepers after a game. I never used to like it when I played. If you've made a mistake you know you've made a mistake, so we just let the situation calm down. After a couple of days I'll speak to the individual and we'll have a look at a video of the game in the coaches' office. I can show them a particular incident from all different angles to illustrate what they've done wrong. They accept the points more when you show them the evidence."

Maintaining a high level of concentration is integral to any goal-keeper's game and that is enhanced greatly by sessions with vision scientist Gail Stephenson during which the stoppers work with the club's hand–eye coordination equipment.

"The sessions with Gail do a lot to keep the players switched on when they're mentally tired," explains Coton. "I remember ex-Liverpool goalkeeper Ray Clemence letting in only sixteen goals in one title-winning season. He'd usually have only one save to make per game and it would often be in the last ten minutes, but he would still be switched on to things despite having had very little to do prior to that. You have to emphasise the importance of concentration to the keepers and Gail certainly helps with that. I always tell them 'if you have to be unemployed, be unemployed, don't go looking for work that's not there.'"

The hand–eye coordination machine is just one of a number of top-of-the-range pieces of equipment the players have at their disposal within the confines of Carrington. A fully equipped gym with a cardio-vascular section, and a weights section with free weights and resistance machinery are all on offer, as are balance training machines and an agility machine that the players use to hone their reaction skills.

"Dots come on the screen and they have to jump around on the floor, a bit like those dancing machines," explains Rob Swire, who became United's head physiotherapist in 1999. "Balance, strength, agility and flexibility are very important for the players. Flexibility is fairly straightforward, you just stretch. Agility, balance and strength are extremely important and they need to be worked on, so we have some specific equipment to train these aspects of fitness."

Additionally, there are the 30 spinning bikes which the squad tend to use before training. A 25-metre indoor swimming pool (which is also made available for community use on Wednesdays and Thursdays as part of the club's link-up with Trafford Borough Council), jacuzzi, steam room and sauna offer the players a variety of relaxation options after training. The pool itself is often used to aid recovery from injury, as is the unique water treadmill, which the club had installed during the 2006/07 season.

"We use it a lot with the injured players," says Rob, who travels everywhere with the first team. "It takes some of the body weight off, which means a player can use it much earlier than the normal treadmill or running outside. It can get players back into normal patterns of movement with a lot less pressure on the injury, which can help them return to fitness quicker.

"As part of the rehabilitation of injuries, you want to stress the damaged tissue slightly and gradually increase this stress back to normal levels. Too much force can break it down, but if you just sit and

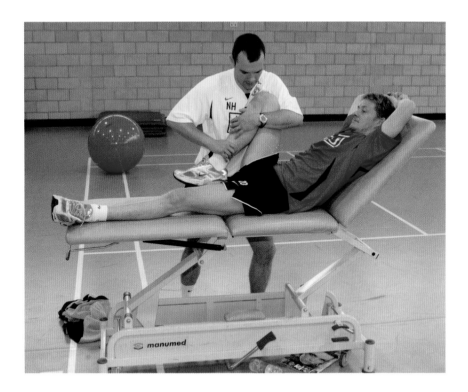

Assistant head
physiotherapist Neil
Hough gets to work on
Ole Gunnar Solskjaer.

wait, it takes a long time. So you try and stress it in the appropriate way to stimulate the healing. That's where some of the advantages of the equipment we are lucky to have at our disposal can come in. The water treadmill can help us to modify the full normal forces, so that the players can still be active without putting too much stress on the injury, and we can increase the force gradually throughout the rehabilitation.

"We try and make sure we have the best equipment and facilities available," he adds. "My role involves keeping up to date with advances in treatment and rehabilitation which requires detailed reading, searching the internet and talking to people with various expertise."

"Because we've got very open-minded coaches and staff, we've always got the latest equipment," adds Louis Saha. "Every new thing for fitness is here and it's always good to try things out to find out their benefits. I always take the chance to have a look at new inventions and I very much enjoy it."

One man particularly familiar with the Carrington medical facilities is Ole Gunnar Solskjaer. The Norwegian endured a torrid time during his recovery from a long-term knee injury which kept him out of action

Physio Rob Swire is called into action to tend to Nemanja Vidic.

for over 18 months between May 2004 and December 2005. The hugely popular Reds' striker made an impressive full return to action during the title-winning 2006/07 season, netting 11 goals in the process. He says he will be eternally grateful for the support he received from United's medical team, who were never short of encouragement during what was a truly wretched period.

"I've got nothing but praise for the physios and medical staff because they carried me through," admits Solskjaer, who is now a coach at the club having been forced to retire from the game because of injury in August 2007. "Being mentally ready is just as important as the physical side, because you have to be ready to go through the hard work that comes with your recovery and we worked on that together. I asked for a week off here and there, and they gave it to me whenever I wanted. The club provided me with everything I needed during that time."

The men primarily entrusted with nursing the players back to full fitness are Rob Swire and club doctor Steve McNally. They are aided and abetted by a host of fellow medics who are all specialists in their respective fields. There are five physios in total at the club – Rob, assistant head physiotherapist Neil Hough (who accompanies Rob on first team trips), John Davin (who travels with the Reserves) and Richard Merron (who attends every Academy game) who all work with the full-time players, a group which consists of around 60 to 70 professionals. Additionally, Mandy Johnson, assisted by four part-time physios, looks after the 150 part-time Academy players.

Mike Clegg works closely with the full-time physios in his role as strength and conditioning coach, while the club's two masseurs, Garry Armer and Rod Thornley, also work with the first team players. Fellow doctor Tony Gill helps McNally cover the entire playing staff at the club, while additional medical help comes from podiatrist Steve Lyons and dietician Trevor Lea.

It's a highly distinguished team and one that plays an integral role in the team's ultimate fate on the pitch. Regular early risers, the majority of the physiotherapy team are stationed at their Carrington desks by 7 a.m. in preparation for the players' arrival and morning training session.

"It's predominantly to avoid the traffic!" jokes Rob Swire. "We all live quite a long way away, so it's convenient for us to get in early and have some breakfast. The physios and the club doctor will then plan the day ahead with what we think we'll be doing with the injured players. Then, just before the players arrive, we'll go and see the coaches to discuss what the fit players will be doing that day. That might have a bearing on whether a player is involved or not; if he's already carrying a slight knock he may not join in a heavy training session. So we liaise with the coaches and find out who's in and who's out, so that we all know what's happening and the coaches can finalise their training programmes.

"I'll then head to the first team dressing room and work with the fit players up until they start training which is usually at 10 a.m. I'll check out minor injuries and sort out strappings, stretches and manual treatments. Once the squad are out on the pitch, I then start working with the injured players. We reassess every injury every day before a player does anything, allowing us to finalise the treatment and rehabilitation.

"After the team finish training, I'll be back in the dressing room to sort out any knocks that they may have picked up during the session. My role is split between monitoring and treating the fit and injured players; it's not just about looking after the injured ones like many people think. I usually continue working with the injured players after lunch and I also meet up with the coaches again so we can update each other on the day's events and the situation with the injured ones. It's important that the coaching staff and the physios have a good link-up so everyone knows what's happening. A lot of my job involves coordinating the communication between all the members of the medical team and the coaches, and passing information back and forth between everybody."

Ensuring there is an unwavering bond of trust between patient and medic can be crucial to a player's recovery and rehabilitation.

"They have to trust you, otherwise they may not tell you the full details of their injuries," reasons Rob. "Obviously we have to liaise with the manager and the coaches but the players understand that. You have to be confidential with certain matters. For instance, if you think an injury is going to affect the availability of a player for matches, then you have to let the manager and coaches know, and the players understand that. You discuss that with the player first, and then tell the manager once you have the player's permission.

"A good manager will trust his medical staff to deal with injuries and won't expect all the information from players to be passed onto them. As long as the manager feels the injuries are being dealt with professionally, I always find that the medical staff are left to look after things as they see fit. That's always been the case with Sir Alex, although I believe it's not always the case at other clubs.

"Similarly with the coaches, they understand that not everything is passed on to them; you're allowed to use your discretion. If a player is going to be fit to play, there's no need to say anything more. If your decision is that he's going to be fit, even if he's got a little this or a little that, it doesn't matter. They're either fit or they're not. You can keep some things confidential which the players like. They don't want to be seen to always have something wrong with them. They might have five little things wrong, but if they're still going to play, there's no point revealing that. Things can be difficult at times but I've survived Sir Alex, some world-class players and one or two tricky characters over more than sixteen years now, so I must be doing something right."

The satisfaction of seeing a player cross that white line once more, after a spell on the sidelines, is a huge one for United's medical staff. But it's ultimately a feeling that is tinged with concern in case there is a recurrence of the original complaint.

"You're always a bit worried about that when a player comes back from injury," admits club doctor Steve McNally, who arrived at United from Liverpool after the tour of South Africa in July 2006. "Hopefully though, if we've planned the rehabilitation progression carefully, then the risk of that happening should be diminished.

"At times you will accept a calculated risk and our role then is an advisory one to the player, manager and the coaching staff. We try to give them as much objective information as we can so they can make a fully informed subjective decision. Sometimes situations dictate that players have to play when they're not one hundred per cent fit. Towards the latter stages of the season there are very few players who are fully fit, unless they've just come back from a long-term injury picked up earlier in the campaign.

Club doctor Steve McNally helps broken nose victim Edwin van der Sar off the pitch at White Hart Lane.

"There are different challenges for the medical staff at different stages of the season," he adds. "Competing on a number of fronts during the final part of the season can be very challenging – there is an increase in the number of games the team play and there's often a lot travelling involved. And, of course, the more games you play, the more contact injuries you're likely to pick up and more fatigue injuries can also occur."

While the physiotherapy staff determine the fine detail of a player's rehabilitation process, McNally is on hand to help boost the mental state of an injured party.

"The psychological side is just as important as the physical aspect," he says. "I try to create a positive atmosphere during my consultations with the players and we always try to maintain the best disposition possible within the treatment room environment irrespective of what's happened on the football side. You've got to remember you're treating the individual first and foremost within the context of the team set-up and all the pressures that they have to deal with. A club doctor's primary

Wes Brown tries out one of the pieces of machinery that ensures United stay at the forefront.

responsibility is always to the individual player. There will be different needs for each player according to differing ages, expectations, cultures and previous experiences – all sorts of factors influence the management of patients at a football club just as they do in healthcare in any other sphere.

"I've always tried to provide players with an understanding of the mechanics of their injury – why it's happened, what structures have been involved, and what their role is in terms of football specific movements. I then discuss why it's important to do certain things and avoid others. This will hopefully provide them with a better understanding of their rehabilitation and the realistic timescale to recovery. I like to show the players their scans because images are often a good way of explaining things, particularly if there are language difficulties.

"There can be significant variability in players' moods and frame of mind during the rehabilitation process and there can be any number of reasons for that," he continues. "Something may be affecting them in their private life or they may have had a reaction to the work we've been doing with them as a necessary exercise challenge. They may also feel frustrated if the team are doing well but they're not able to be involved at that point. Players obviously want to get back playing as soon as possible."

McNally's role at the club is a somewhat varied one which involves fulfilling a range of administrative duties on top of his practical obligations.

"I do a lot of screening examinations and life insurance medicals," he explains. "Individual players and the club arrange insurance policies that require medical examinations and reports and they are part of my remit. I also assist in educational and welfare aspects for the scholars and I'm involved in Health and Safety issues, particularly those that have an impact on the players.

"The medical department is continually auditing and reviewing its practices and we are involved in wider injury audits in conjunction with UEFA. We undertake our own clinical research and partake in other research projects that will develop our understanding of athletic injury and health issues further. I am inundated with information from equipment manufacturers, pharmaceutical companies and other organisations in the athletic healthcare field and I have to assess the potential usefulness of any innovative treatment interventions, discuss them with the medical team and the players, and make a business case for incorporating changes if we feel that we could benefit from them and gain a competitive advantage.

"I find Ultrasound scanning very useful in the initial assessment [of an injury] and as a monitoring tool during recovery from muscle and tendon injuries. We don't have X-ray facilities at Carrington, but we generally don't do many anyway. They're really only used to diagnose a fracture in an acute situation or to monitor fracture healing, but even then we'd often use more sophisticated technology like CT [computed tomography] or MRI [magnetic resonance imaging] scanning. We have very good access to investigations at some of the private hospitals in Manchester with whom we have developed good relations, and I always accompany players to specialist appointments where key diagnostic or treatment intervention decisions are to be made.

"I'm also often asked for some advice or a second opinion by staff members from all departments on personal health issues," adds Steve. "While not strictly part of the job, it is flattering that staff feel able to approach me, and it is part of the family atmosphere that exists within the club, particularly at Carrington."

Diet continues to play an ever-important role in an athlete's make-up. For that reason, Steve liaises regularly with dietician Trevor Lea regarding any individual dietary modifications that may be required during a player's injury or illness recovery.

"It's all about matching the energy that goes into a player's body through the food he eats to that which goes out," explains Trevor, a United employee since August 1992. "If a player is used to training five times a week and also playing two or three games within that period then he's getting rid of a lot of calories, and eating a matching amount. If all of a sudden he's injured and won't be training for a couple of weeks then he doesn't need anywhere near the number of calories he's been eating. So he'll need advice on how he can cut back.

"The human body gets into habits of eating certain amounts. Our weight stays pretty stable because we generally eat the same – certainly on a weekly basis. There's a very good control mechanism in the body, just to eat what we need. If you change that input for a couple of weeks you might lose or gain a stone, but it stays remarkably stable if your lifestyle's the same. But if you suddenly stop exercising, you still carry on wanting to eat the same amount, that's why each player needs to change their eating habits.

"Vitamin and mineral deficiencies can slow down healing, but at the same time you can't speed up healing by eating excesses. If you've not got enough of a certain substance maybe it'll take longer to repair, but eating ten times the amount won't make you recover ten times faster. Otherwise it would be like something off *Star Trek* where somebody has a fracture and they wave that stick over it and it goes 'whiiiiirrrrrp'. If only that were true. Players wouldn't be out for so long! As I said, it's about matching what each player eats to their training, and as their training starts to increase they can start to eat more until they're back to normal amounts."

Trevor works closely with the Carrington chefs on a daily basis to create suitable menu choices for Old Trafford's finest footballers.

"I quite enjoy recipe development," says Trevor, who also coordinates the food options for United's travelling party during domestic and European away trips and pre-season tours. "It can involve thinking of new recipes or taking an old one which is high in fat and low in carbs and making it more balanced, in terms of what a footballer needs. If you eat in a restaurant you're eating for taste, which often includes large amounts of fat, oil, cheese and cream. This tastes great and you go away feeling very full, but that's not the objective for a footballer. They're eating for performance.

"As a matter of principle a person stands a better chance of getting good nutrition if they eat a bigger variety of foods. If you're eating varied fruits, vegetables and salads, you get a greater diversity of vitamins, minerals and trace elements. It's therefore important to keep trying new and different foods. I like to encourage variety, that way you never get too much of a bad thing. I particularly encourage the players to eat more fish and meals containing peas, beans and lentils.

"For many years a high protein diet was in fashion [for players]," continues Trevor. "I've spoken to footballers who played up to fifty years ago and they were encouraged to eat meat when possible, the idea being that this would build them up and give them lots of energy. But research has shown that a high protein diet is not the best for a footballer. The emphasis now is on achieving a correct balance of energy-giving foods, with particular inclusion of fruit, vegetables and salads which enable natural absorption into the body of vitamins, minerals and trace elements. These help with energy production in the muscles, as well as with recovery from matches, training and repair of injury."

So what do the players like to munch on after a morning session on the training pitch?

"Chicken curry is always a winner," reveals Trevor. "Some players would eat that every day! Low-fat chicken curry, that is, made our way. Fish fingers and fishcakes are also popular; we get through a lot of those – particularly the homemade fishcakes. Pizza – homemade, deep-base for your carbohydrates is another favourite. Toppings include chicken, spicy beef, or tuna and sweet corn. But again they're not high in fat. We don't smother them in cheese.

United dietician Trevor Lea shows how fruit can have more than one use.

"Sometimes it doesn't go down so well that what's on offer is always low fat. It's a challenge to take all the flavour and fat out of a dish until it's bland and tasteless, and then give it to the players – but that's exactly my job. That's what the players say, that's my reputation, and it's pretty accurate to be fair! The real challenge is to make low-fat food tasty and have the right texture. We experiment a lot with different textures and herbs and other ways of getting taste in. Players are allowed fat and they need fat – every human being does, there are some fats which are essential for the human body – that's why I'm always banging on about oily fish and green leafy vegetables.

"Of course players can go home and eat a lot of fat, I can't follow them home. But they themselves don't really like eating too much fat because it means they start to slow down. They're very conscious of that. Football is very competitive nowadays and they're very keen on looking after their bodies. With the frequency of games, you've got to be in pretty good shape to keep up."

Trevor insists there is no formulaic nutritional regime that suits all footballers. Assessing players on an individual basis, particularly the club's foreign imports, is essential to them following a healthy and beneficial diet.

"My advice depends more on the individual's lifestyle and metabolism," explains Trevor. "You could have two players in the same position,

but one's lifestyle and eating pattern is totally different to the other, and their metabolism can be different as well. Some players might like three big meals, while others might prefer four small snacks. There isn't one perfect diet – of course, that goes for everybody in the world, not just footballers.

"Foreign players are used to eating the foods from their own country. My job is to try to explain to them that they aren't going to get them – in a nice way, of course! I explain to them what's in English foods and persuade them to try little bits of different things. They eventually learn to eat our foods. The worst thing is if a player doesn't like mushrooms, say, and they have a dish and taste mushrooms, then they say 'ugh, English food is awful.' It just takes time to get used to it. In fairness, we do a variety of international dishes here anyway. Standard things like Coq au Vin, low-fat chicken stir fry and curries. We just work with them to get them used to English foods and the way we cook things.

"There are many ways to get a balanced diet," he continues. "So I try to work out what would be balanced for each individual player and give specific advice. If you give a diet sheet to somebody they'll follow it for a few days, but if it doesn't fit in with their lifestyle then they won't stick to it for a long time. You have to tailor individual plans."

OUT OF HOURS

4

Howls of laughter ring out from the Carrington first team changing room. The players are sporadically making their way inside the main building after their morning training session, but one unlucky victim has returned to the sight of his clothes hanging up in full view of everyone – a sure sign that his team-mates rate today's wardrobe selection as a fashion disaster.

"Edwin [van der Sar] used to get done about his clothes all the time but he's begun to play it safe," reveals Rio Ferdinand. "When he was here, Henrik Larsson's shoes were put up on the bench quite a lot; we never saw the pair he wore on his first day at training ever again after

The Carrington changing room, were the wrong clothes are always at risk.

Albert Morgan gets little sympathy from Sir Alex after losing another item of his clothing to the players' tricks.

that! Ronny [Cristiano Ronaldo] isn't impressed if you single out any of his things because he thinks his stuff is the best."

"It's happened to me a couple of times!" jokes Wayne Rooney. "Louis [Saha] probably gets the brunt of it, his clothes are awful! There's always something happening among the lads, so you always need to think twice about what you're doing and where you are."

Trying to unearth the main culprit and his accomplices is not always easy given the array of suspects, although Rooney and Ronaldo are usually high on everyone's list. Ole Gunnar Solskjaer, however, has an alternative theory.

"I'm not sure the players are always to blame," he insists. "Things often happen when we're out training so my guess is it's the staff – there are a few bad 'uns among them! Rod Thornley, one of the masseurs, is usually involved. He's got too much time on his hands!

"Rod once frightened the life out of Phil Neville," chips in Rio. "He got inside Phil's locker and when he came in from training and opened it Rod jumped out and screamed. Phil was absolutely terrified!

"Wazza [Wayne Rooney] and Ronny are always up to something and Fletch [Darren Fletcher] has also come into the equation. He once put dye in Wes's [Brown] shoes which was hilarious. Patrice Evra always loves a joke. But he's often the butt of a lot of them because he's so small – Wazza and Ronny give him some serious stick about his height!"

"There's always been banter among the players, even from when I first joined the club," continues Solskjaer. "That's never diminished. Each player adds something different to the dressing room which is great. You have to be able to take a joke – if someone gets you hook, line and sinker then you just have to laugh at it."

Aside from catching out their team-mates, the players also target the coaching staff with their pranks.

"You learn to be on your guard when there are things going down with the lads," insists kit manager Albert Morgan. "Some of their favourite tricks include cutting the crotch out of your underpants or cutting the end off your socks. But the ones that have done that have soon regretted it!

"Cristiano has come into his own as the joker of the camp – he's come from nowhere! I love Ronny – he's done very well for the club and is a great lad. Scholesy can be a little bugger when he wants – you can never trust Scholesy.

"All the lads are fantastic and there is great banter between them and the coaching staff. It helps to keep you young and it certainly helped me recover from my heart surgery a few years ago. The players all came to see me at the hospital with planks of wood asking me which one I fancied for my coffin! That kind of banter keeps you going."

Kit assistant John Campbell, who has been at the club since 1993, is a daily victim.

"John is always getting stick from someone, if not myself then Wazza or Ronny," reveals Ferdinand. "There isn't a day that goes by without that happening. There is a brilliant atmosphere around the whole training ground, not just among the players and the coaching staff but with the girls in the general office and the chefs in the canteen. We all have a good laugh together."

Another source of amusement, albeit one tinged with a competitive edge, is the players' basketball competition. The NBA wannabes usually consist of Wayne Rooney, Rio Ferdinand, Wes Brown, Nemanja Vidic, Darren Fletcher and Tomasz Kuszczak. A shooting game, dubbed "One Bounce" by the group, or a mini tournament involving three-on-three or four-on-four scenarios make up the usual routine. "One Bounce" sees each player take aim at the hoop and score points for each successful shot. After each attempt the ball is allowed to bounce once but you have to shoot from wherever the ball is picked up after the first bounce.

"You might end up twenty metres away or you could be right next to the basket," explains Rio.

"You basically shoot until you miss and whoever is next in line can pick up the rebound. It's then their turn to shoot," chips in Fletcher. "You get different points for shooting from different areas."

"Vida [Nemanja Vidic] is a pretty good player but Wes has won more games than anyone else," continues Rio. "He used to play at school and he's also got a net in his garden so he practises all the time at home which gives him a slight advantage. He's probably the best player out of all of us, even though it hurts me to say it!"

"At first Wes was miles ahead of everyone," admits Fletcher. "But like Rio says, that was mainly because he has a net at home to practise with.

Now we're all catching up with him. Tomasz is the only one who can execute a proper slam dunk. He shows off a bit about that but he can't shoot so we give him plenty of stick!"

"He might be good at dunking but Tomasz has absolutely no idea about the rules!" quips Rio, who is just as prolific with a bat and a ping-pong ball at his fingertips. "Me and Ronny are probably the best at table tennis," he adds defiantly. "Quinton Fortune used to be pretty decent when he was here and Ben Foster isn't bad, but Ronny and I have a little battle going now."

Another highly contested battle revolves around the Carrington prediction league. Started in 2002 by Carrington head groundsman Joe Pemberton, there are usually over 20 members of staff who don their football prophecy hats on a weekly basis, including Sir Alex and some of the players such as Ole Gunnar Solskjaer, Darren Fletcher and Wes Brown. The gaffer, who has seen a number of his players collect a wooden spoon – handed out for finishing in the bottom five – remains suspicious about the legitimacy of the forecasting process.

"I'm sure there's something going on," he jokes. "It's always the girls in the office that are winning it – I think they put their predictions in on Saturday nights after the results come through!"

Training may often be over by noon, but the players still have various

Goalkeeper Ben Foster
turns his hand to
a different sport.

commitments to fulfil before their working day ends. A cluster head off to the gym to meet with strength and conditioning coach Mike Clegg, who devises a special programme for the players to follow to build up their body strength, while others go for a massage or partake in a spot of yoga – Ryan Giggs and Mikael Silvestre are regulars. Some have media duties to carry out, often with MUTV, who have a state-of-the-art studio at Carrington, or the club's in-house media team, who produce the official website, matchday programme and magazine.

Others may have sponsorship appearances or community visits to make. Though not always publicised, the players lend a sizeable portion of their time and support to a number of community and charity campaigns, via the Manchester United Foundation, throughout the season. And, according to Rio Ferdinand, it's a responsibility all the lads are more than happy to fulfil.

"We all want to do what we can to give something back to the local community," he says. "I always remember thinking when I was a youngster, I wish someone I'd admired had come to see me and my friends and given us some advice about various things in life. It could have altered the way a lot of my mates thought and stopped them from getting into trouble with the law. If they'd have had the right guidance or inspiration then that might have happened, so I'm keen to do what I can."

One of the ways in which Rio, in particular, is trying to reach out to young people is through his music label White Chalk. Set up by himself and two friends, White Chalk (which has studios in Manchester and London) already has a number of budding performers and producers on its books, as well as good commercial links with a number of UK-renowned companies. Most importantly for the United defender, however, are the label's wide-reaching plans to tap into local communities in a bid to give youngsters a better chance in life.

"We're planning to work with the Manchester United Foundation on various campaigns and give young people who want to get into the music business the opportunity to learn how things work in a studio," explains Rio, who devotes as much time to raising the profile of the label as his Reds' career allows him. "Not every kid is going to be a singer, but that doesn't mean they can't learn how to DJ or how to become a music technician.

"I've now set up my own Foundation called 'Live The Dream' and my aim is to create a number of different centres across the country where kids can go and get involved in football, music or anything in the entertainment field. If they've got an ambition in life hopefully we can help them fulfil it."

Aside from his musical interests, Rio has also shown an eye for TV presenting following his *World Cup Wind-Ups* show that was screened in June 2006. Taking on a Jeremy Beadle-style role, the centre back played tricks on a host of his United and England team-mates and popularised the phrase "You got murked" in much the same way that Demi Moore's other half Ashton Kutcher has "Punk'd" people in his MTV prank show. One of Rio's victims was team-mate Wayne Rooney, whose fiancée Coleen McLoughlin was also in on the act.

"Coleen had been asking me for a few days if I'd go with her to a dogs' home she was doing some work with," recalls Wayne. "I kept saying no because I had something on in Liverpool, but she eventually got me to go. Once I was there loads of weird things started happening."

Indeed they did. First, a plaque was unveiled with Rooney's name misspelt (they had him down as Wayne Ronnie) and then a vet forced the United striker to hold a drip which was attached to a little boy's dog that was supposedly undergoing surgery.

"The vet went out of the room for a second and the dog's monitor flatlined," continues Ferdinand. "The vet came back in and said, 'What's happened?' Wayne said, 'I don't know.' Coleen was laughing her head off in the background."

"I remember thinking thanks for getting me into this Coleen!" adds Wayne. "I have to say it was a good joke though. I haven't got Rio back yet, but I'm sure I will."

There is a queue of players lining up to exact revenge on the Reds' Peckham-born defender, not least club captain Gary Neville whose "murking" Rio rates as his favourite.

"Gaz's response was absolutely unbelievable, it was priceless," laughs Ferdinand, who had two policemen approach Gary, who was with team-mate Ryan Giggs, regarding a series of alleged traffic offences. "The officers were willing to let Gary off if he posed for a photograph with them, but he wasn't budging. Anyone else in the world would have done it, especially if it prevented them from getting six points on their licence, but typical Gaz wouldn't let it be. I'm not worried about the lads getting me back because I don't think anyone's good enough to get me!"

The banter in the United camp rages on, and as well as keeping everyone on their toes, it also builds bonds which ultimately prove telling on the pitch. They all play hard and work hard as a team.

"The team spirit is just fantastic," says Louis Saha. "We all stick together and there are no cowards who shy away from situations. The fact that everyone is committed to the club means we all have some-thing in common. Sometimes things go wrong but that helps the atmosphere as well because everyone wants to go forward together."

The United Academy
at Carrington.

Part Two

YOUTH DEVELOPMENT

"Our responsibility to the future of this game is to give budding talent the very best opportunity to flourish. The Academy is just such a place, a proving ground for tomorrow's heroes." **UNITED ACADEMY PLAQUE**

A RICH TRADITION

5

Should anybody require proof of the unwavering stock United place in their youth system, digest this fact: the club's all-time top four appearance-makers have all come through it. Sir Bobby Charlton, Ryan Giggs, Bill Foulkes and Gary Neville each rose up the Old Trafford ranks before achieving legendary status in football. The names keep coming. Duncan Edwards, George Best, David Beckham and Paul Scholes are just a few more football luminaries who have graced the game in the red of United. And not one of them cost a penny, instead rising through – you guessed it – the club's famously fruitful youth structure.

Some of the young boys training at Carrington – talent-spotting is starting increasingly early these days.

"The Busby Babes" and "Fergie's Fledglings" – as dubbed by the media's catchy title brigade – are an indelible part of United's history, and the most glaring examples of the club's success in developing home-grown talent.

Time has brought changes to the process, of course, most obviously with the advent of the Premier League's 1998 inception of the Academy system, but the principles remain the same. The best young players catch the eye, make the grade and try to clamber to the very top.

Boys can end up representing one of the club's ten Academy teams through being scouted or impressing on trial at one of 24 Development Centres – all of which are located within an hour's drive of Carrington.

Academy rules dictate that a club can only sign a youth player who lives within a certain radius of a nominated main centre – in United's case the Carrington complex. For ages 9–13 the distance is 60 miles, rising to 90 miles for those 14 and over. To paint a picture of how encumbering the rule is, had it been in place 15 years ago then David Beckham would not have been able to join United, and he would have signed with a London team.

"There are a lot of rules and regulations which hinder Manchester United, but you don't have any choice but to abide by them," shrugs Brian McClair, installed as United's Academy manager at the start of the 2006/07 season and the man in charge of enlisting and cultivating the best young talent around.

"We can only continue to bang our drum for what we'd like to see happen. Time and time again our thinking is that the best players won't get better if they're not involved with the best players and best coaches, and nobody will disprove that."

The necessity to spot the most talented youngsters at an increasingly early age makes McClair's job infinitely harder.

"You're looking at babies, really, six or seven years of age and you're trying to evaluate if they have the potential of being elite sportspeople, which is impossible," he says. "I think you just look for basic things, but you're trying to be a soothsayer and project these boys ten years into the future. Genetics play a part so you can have a look at the physical attributes of the parent or parents who bring them along. If the mother's tall then that's good because the son will usually end up at least as tall as

her. You can judge how their hand–eye coordination is. I think you can also tell the character of the boys. Football's made up of lots of different types of players in lots of different positions now, but you might spot someone who's quick over a long distance or short distance. You're looking at all sorts of different factors, but as I say it's very difficult."

Once the players are officially enlisted – with scholarship forms at the age of 16 – it becomes a case of developing them as players and people. McClair and his staff are set on not only equipping their charges for a career in football, but also rounding them socially.

Education Officer Dave Bushell is the main man when it comes to the schooling of United's youngsters once they sign with the club.

"In the early days, we do liaise with their schools, but only with a very light touch," says Bushell. "We make sure the schools know they're with our Academy as such and that they are potentially elite sportspeople.

When they're fourteen things get a little more serious and we send the schools two letters a year just to keep them up to speed on the player's progress.

"If they're good enough players they're offered a scholarship at sixteen, that's Year Eleven in schools. They're offered a job at the club, part of which is an Apprenticeship in Sporting Excellence, which is a scholarship for sports people; in football it is run by the Premier League Learning, an offshoot of the Premier League.

"They're picked for the scholarship on football ability, not on their education. Their academic ability determines which programme we run them through, and the apprenticeship they undertake has three areas.

"The most important aspect of it is the football practical side; that's their training, technical, tactical, physical and mental work they do on the pitch and in the gym. By way of back-up to that, there's now an NVQ programme which is a football diary the boys complete. That's called the FDPD or Football Development Programme Diary, which again is organised by the Premier League.

"In that, they review the work they're doing, set targets for themselves and show how they're going to work on improving themselves. On the field the aspects are technical, tactical, physical and mental.

"Technically, they might target how to improve their control, passing, heading, shooting or whatever, and work on their skills. Tactically, they try to improve their awareness dependent on their position. Physically, they could be working on their pace, upper body strength, spring, as well as a general programme; while mentally, they work on improving concentration.

"They target how to improve each one. They work out things they're not very good at and try to improve them. Then they work out what they're good at and try to get even better."

In addition to a well-rounded football education to improve the players' chances of making the grade and forging a career in the game, United's programme also stands the boys in good stead in case they fall short, preparing them for whichever path they end up travelling in life.

"As well as the football education there are four units in the NVQ which are, if you like, back-up units," says Bushell. "One is health and safety – learning that there are health and safety rules, how to implement them and how they are responsible people.

"There's a unit on lifestyle which fills them in on how to sleep and eat properly – although that's in physical conditioning as well – and outlines basically just how to live properly if you want to be a young footballer of the highest standard.

"Another section is communication, which is geared towards preparing them for dealing with the general public, each other, coaches and peers, as well as a part on media where we work a little bit with MUTV.

"Finally there's also one on career management. That's managing your career at this moment in time in football, managing your career if you don't make it in football but stay on in some other capacity like coaching or physio, and managing it if it goes outside football.

"As well as that, they complete a Technical Certificate. That's their education back-up which is usually in the form of BTECs or AS level courses. We usually end up with them doing BTECs. They're modular and involve project work, which makes it easier for them to jump back into the classroom if they've been on international duty. They can actually do something that links towards their BTEC while they're away. Boys who are very bright push on and do an A level. For example, Jonny Evans did an AS level in Maths and Ben Amos is doing an A level in English Language.

Youngsters have the facilities for learning at Carrington, in the Academy building classroom, but also spend one and a half days per week attending the club's partner school in Ashton-On-Mersey, spending Monday mornings and all day Thursday in classes working on their BTECs.

Education the Manchester United way inevitably incorporates history lessons about the club's traditions, while Carrington's Academy building is adorned with visual reminders of the players who have worn the well-trodden path through United's ranks.

"We do, as much as possible, try to educate them and give them bites of what it's been like in youth development in the last fifty-odd years at Manchester United," says McClair. "I think the older they get you can drip in more things.

"There are also photographs up in the Academy building of players

Brian McClair takes a training session with the Reserves, (L-R) Kieran Lee, Michael Lea, Danny Simpson and Sean Evans.

who have come through the development system before them. We also set them little projects to find out about football in general and Manchester United in particular."

The main aim of taking on youngsters is – of course – to improve their on-field abilities, a target which is achieved through a number of facets.

"All the way through kids learn by enjoying themselves," says McClair. "We want them to have fun and we want them to love the game. If they love the game they'll want to practise it.

"We try to play games of four against four as much as we can. It has been proven scientifically that the kids get so many more touches of the ball and get in situations like one against one, or two against one, than they would in games of eight v eight or eleven v eleven. That's just common sense, and we continue to batter on about it because we think it's the right way to help the kids learn."

More contact with the ball places youngsters in more and more situations that require problem solving and, in Rene Meulensteen, United have a coach who can equip the kids with all the lock-picking tips they need.

The Dutchman is back in his second spell with the club after a six-month foray into top-flight management with Brondby. Upon deciding to leave Denmark, Meulensteen was delighted to reassume his original role of technical skills coach at Carrington. Rene's role is to give all the players – from the fresh-faced youths right up to the grizzled first-team veterans – the wherewithal to emerge victorious from any one-on-one situation anywhere on a football pitch. A devout student of the work of famed coach Wiel Coerver, Meulensteen spent five years working with his fellow Dutchman on a daily basis with the Qatar FA before he came to United in 2001.

"I first got in touch with Wiel's work in 1985," says Rene, who also managed the Reserves to a memorable treble in 2006. "His first book was *The Learning Plan For The Ideal Player* which introduced different skills and turns. The thing that struck me was the preface and introduction, the reasoning behind it all, and I thought it was spot on. The analysis was so sharp. He identified all the important aspects shown by the best players. You didn't have to be a genius to understand it. I always believed in his philosophy, I still do. In that respect everything he said then is still very much true in the modern game.

"For me it's a big, exciting challenge to prove he's right perhaps, at a big club like United. Not only possibly with the youngsters coming through, but with an immediate impact with the first team. That's a great challenge. He's been a massive influence on me. The only thing I've done is try to capture it in a slightly different way to share it with other people."

The basic premise of Meulensteen's approach is to make young players more skilful, confident and dominant on the field. With a cocktail of honed drills and astute psychology, he arms United's Academy sides with what is essentially a toolbox of trickery.

"You need to be able to draw from as many options as possible," he says. "One-touch play, unpredictable running off the ball, dummy runs, turns, standing still, different speeds, all so that the opposing defender is thinking 'what the hell is he going to do next?' That's the point you want to be at, and once you're there, that's when you dominate. The funny bit about that is that these things are the least highlighted, in general. How many Cristiano Ronaldos are running around the Premier

Rene Meulensteen insists:
'Let's make the players as
skilful as we can from a
very young age.'

League? Yes, he's got a great natural gift, but very, very few players have the core ability to turn in different ways and change the angle of their attacks. That's because it's not being trained, that's the whole issue.

"To solve that problem, you have to make it an important part of your development programme – which we do here. I think it was United themselves who identified that they needed to add something to their development programme within the Academy in terms of skills development, and that's what I've tried to implement. That was my brief from the beginning: let's make the players as skilful as we can from a very young age. You could take one player from five of our youth teams and ask each one to show you a move to beat a man. They could all do it, because we've exposed them to it and trained them to do it.

"If you can make a player good technically, and then over the years develop other aspects, then you'll see a different kind of animal coming through, someone who can beat an opponent without thinking. It's not just skill though, personality and attitude carry the skill."

What quickly becomes apparent from sitting with Meulensteen for any prolonged period is the stock he places in psychology, and he readily admits it is a vital tool in getting the best out of footballers.

"Sometimes with the very young teams you see players just dribbling with the ball until they lose it and I don't care, because it's about affecting their attitude," he says. "I want them to have no fear. The adults might be at the side of the pitch shouting 'pass', but that's their decision. If the boy then passes the ball, it's no good because it's not his decision. You want him to pass the ball himself. If he does then great, it shows good vision, so it's the game between nature and nurture. What's there and how do we develop it?

"With that kind of skill level you need a certain style to play. With each individual Reserves player in the 2005/06 season I encouraged them to make a difference with what they were good at. I enjoyed it because every time I watched them play, most of the time it was exciting to watch. It was high tempo, there was the six-nil win over Manchester City where everything came together and we blew them away, Fraizer Campbell got four goals and we never took our foot off the pedal, we could have easily scored more."

Before that game, which effectively sealed the first part of the

Reserves' 2005/06 Treble, Meulensteen had calmly strolled up to Campbell during the warm-up. The striker was routinely shooting at the open goal when Rene asked: "Have you picked your spot?" When pressed to explain, the Dutchman pointed out that picking a spot, placing a shot in each corner of the goal, during the warm-up would prove beneficial during the game. Four goals later, his advice had been spectacularly heeded.

"I still do that now with first team players, telling them to pick their spot," Rene smiles. "The mind is such a strong weapon if it works for you. First of all you have to learn how it works. You have a choice to feel how you feel, you have a choice to think what you think. You can think positively or negatively, they're the only choices you've got. It costs equally as much energy, but the benefits of thinking positively are a thousand times greater. What it does is focus.

"I do a lot of finishing exercises where in the corners of the goal I'll put coloured bibs. Instead of just lashing the ball at goal you have to hit the bib. It focuses you. You focus on direction; direction becomes a purpose so when you hit the bib you'll probably score. Simple little psychological things like that calm down the mind and compose you.

"When you pick a spot, the moment you do it then you visualise the ball going in and how you've done it. In every spot you're going to score, visualise a goal. It's like a quick movie in your head. By the time the scenario comes up during a game, you've already been there and seen it go in. I did that with Ruud van Nistelrooy during his time here. I did it with Dong [Fangzhuo] and [Chris] Eagles during the 2006/7 season, shooting with and without the bibs. As soon as you get them aiming for the bibs, the number of goals goes up by about eighty per cent.

"There's so much more to get out of teams and individual players if you affect their minds. We only use less than ten per cent of the brain, which is for the core, simple daily routines. The rest of the brain is untapped, and when you start to tap into it, that's when you can start to shape your own destiny. That's when people start to understand that success and happiness are a choice. Happiness is a state of mind, nothing else. Things that you really want, you will get over time in some shape or form."

Positive thought and unwavering focus is a mindset that Meulensteen tries to drill into every player he works with. Whether they're six or 36, the right psychological approach paves the way for success.

"When there's an influence, there's an emotion which is your positive or negative reaction," he says, reaching for a pen to scribble down another explanatory diagram. "That's your choice. Negativity makes you irritated, frustrated, loses your focus and leads to a bad performance. It drags you down. People who remain positive, stay confident and focused will eventually have a positive performance, and that's the spring. Those are the two routes you can go, red or green. I always encourage players to stay in the green.

"You can change players' behaviour by making them aware of it and making them understand the consequences and the far more beneficial, enjoyable alternative. I used this exact model with the Reserves. I had five clips of [tennis champion] Roger Federer, all lasting six seconds. The first three seconds were a shot; the second three were a close-up of him. The test I gave them was to work out what score it was, what game, what set, what tournament it was.

"I guaranteed them that they'd almost certainly only be able to get the tournament, and even that would be because of the different surfaces he was playing on. They'd only get that one because he always controlled his emotions. He's always positive, always confident, always focused. It's the next ball that matters, nothing else; he never gets carried away even if he hits it out. You can see him sitting on the bench, it doesn't matter what set or score it is. He looks the same.

"Imagine if we could be in that kind of control as footballers? Rather than waste time arguing with the referee, we could be getting back into position and defending. It's all about awareness and understanding."

The results of the work undertaken by Meulensteen and his fellow coaches will not impact on United's first team for years – he's the first to admit that success hinges on senior results – but there are signs through the Academy ranks that the skills mantra is reaping dividends.

"Since starting in 2001, I see the U14s as the spearhead," he says. "They were the U9s then. The older age groups caught a bit of it, but the U9s were the ones we did a lot with. All of them have gone through the same development tunnel, and you can definitely see that now. They're taking technique into skill, into small-sided games, into

strategy. They've got good understanding of the principles of their play, good understanding of their positions, how to commit opponents and how to deal with them.

"You see a lot of really good, exciting football. You see lots of running past players, good turns, beating players, skills; it's exciting for me to watch them. By the time they hit the youth team our skill level will be so much higher than opponents'. A number of them have got the ability to use their skills to their liking. The next few years could be very, very exciting."

For all the effort from the club and the individual players, not every youngster can go on to be a star in the United first team, a sad fact intrinsic of the club's sky-high standards. The end of each season is always a nervy time for United's Academy scholars as they anxiously await the decision of whether or not they will be offered professional

Fraizer Campbell scores the first of his four goals during the Reserves' April 2006 victory over City that effectively sealed the first part of their Treble. 'Pick a spot ... visualise a goal,' advises Meulensteen.

forms and kept on at the club. Breaking the bad news to those who don't make it remains the most unpalatable aspect of Sir Alex Ferguson's duties.

"That's always been the hardest part of my job," says Sir Alex. "It's not easy at all. Fortunately, we don't release that many per year, it's usually about four or five. It's not easy nonetheless, because these young kids have come here with a dream.

"What we try to guarantee most parents is that we can get the boys careers in the game. In the Football League in the 2006/07 season we had forty-six players who had come through our system, which is an incredibly high percentage. In most cases we fulfil our obligation to parents and generally have a high percentage of players who go on to have a career in the game.

"There are players scattered all over the country, in fact three of them played against us for Sheffield United in April 2007. Danny Webber, Keith Gillespie and Michael Tonge all came through our Academy, and you see that right through the country. That gives a satisfaction that we're doing our job reasonably well."

6

THE PROVING GROUND

Visitors to Carrington's Academy building are drawn to a sign on the first floor balcony that reads: "Our responsibility to the future of this game is to give budding talent the very best opportunity to flourish. The Academy is just such a place, a proving ground for tomorrow's heroes."

For those who do make it into the United Academy and receive a professional contract, that's the point where their football education really begins, and they start to learn about life as a Manchester United player.

"When you're coming up through the ranks, everything is geared

The potential stars
of the future at
Carrington.

Danny Welbeck scores
the fourth goal against
Arsenal in April 2007 to
seal his side's place in the
final of the Youth Cup.

towards playing in the first team," says Darren Fletcher, who signed professional forms with United in July 2000. "From your preparation before matches, including what you eat for your pre-match meal, to formations you'd play in training and the style of play – it's all very much geared to the senior squad. It's fantastic to have that approach because it means that when you do make that step up it's a much more smooth transition, rather than going from one extreme to the other."

Fans and families gather to watch the U18s play their home Academy League match at Carrington on Saturday mornings. The gates are invariably meagre by comparison to a bustling Old Trafford, but occasionally, you will find some stars dotted around the crowd.

"If there is an U18s game on a Saturday morning at Carrington and we're training ahead of a Sunday match, a good majority of the lads will walk over and watch the match," admits Fletcher.

The first team often turn out to watch United's youngsters in FA Youth Cup action. While Academy League games are seen as rehearsal situations, the Youth Cup is held in high regard at the club, which won the first five tournaments back in the 1950s.

"When you're younger Youth Cup games are always important," says the Scottish international. "I got the chance to play in the Youth Cup and thoroughly enjoyed the experience. It's always been a special competition to this club, and a lot of the first team players will take time out to go and watch the games. The manager has always taken a keen interest in every match the youngsters play and continues to do so.

"We always keep an eye on which players are coming through and which have a chance of making it into the senior squad. There's a fine line between success and failure, so it's important that, as a young player, you really knuckle down and work hard."

The 2006/07 season saw United appear in a record 13th final, although heartache was the order of the day as Paul McGuinness' side were pipped on penalties by reigning cup-holders Liverpool.

A sterling run provided more than its fair share of enduring memories, not least a stunning, typically Manchester United comeback in the semi-final second leg against Arsenal at Old Trafford. A goal down from the first leg, the Reds fell behind on the night, before roaring back to snatch a 2-1 victory in the fourth minute of stoppage time. Extra

Sir Alex shares a joke
with some of the club's
young hopefuls.

time saw the Reds fall behind on aggregate, but they again countered, with two goals in the final ten minutes, to win the tie 4-3 and book their place in the final. Although ultimately beaten in the final, McGuinness was delighted with his side's run and the proof that the club's onus on Youth Cup success remains as strong as ever.

"The Youth Cup's the competition we really try and get our best team out for all the time," he says. "You look at which team could best win each game. In the other games we don't do that. Of course we want to win them, every team we put out is done so with the aim of winning, part of their development is winning. But there are other factors that come into it.

"If we want to promote players we'll play them in the Reserves, so we won't necessarily be able to play our best team in the U18s. You've also got to be fair to everybody and give them all an opportunity to play. Sometimes the first year scholars will play when, realistically, if we wanted to win every game they wouldn't.

"Schoolboys played in some of our league games last season and got great experience. Certainly we'd like to win the Academy League, but it's not the be-all and end-all. The most important thing is that the players develop through that. In a perfect world, we'd like them to develop while winning it obviously!"

Given that Paul's father Wilf is a former United player and manager, and is still highly involved with the club, it's of little surprise that the U18s manager is particularly mindful of United's tradition of developing young talent.

"I've been brought up on it," he admits. "I think it's a very important thing for our young players to know about it. You see the heart and soul. All the teams that have done well at United have had home-grown players in them. From the Busby Babes, that obviously was a big period, but in the sixties, when they had a revival after Munich, they won the Youth Cup in 1964. George Best, David Sadler, John Aston, Jimmy Rimmer were there, and they all went on to play in the first team. When they won the European Cup in 1968 I think there were eight home-grown players in the side.

"Then again in 1999 there were five or six home-grown players at least, so it's always been at the core of the club's successful periods to

have home-grown players. That's not to say that the big stars who come in do nothing, they're a massive part of it, but the home-grown players create a feel around the place which help the likes of Cantona and Solskjaer fall in love with the club. And, of course, the crowd loves home-grown stars, and there's a big influence of them on the club's history and success. We feel it's important that our players know about that, and hopefully there are one or two of the current lot who will be carrying that on in the future."

As well as educating their boys on United's off-field mantra, the

Paul McGuinness, United's U18 manager, watches from the sidelines during a game early in the 2006/07 season.

Academy's coaches also try to replicate the fast, entertaining style of play on the pitch, which has been the club's hallmark down the years.

"It's the way we work at it from a young age," says McGuinness. "A big part of it then is mixing the age groups. They see the older ones, they start to play with them and then they get a feel for it and a feel for playing the United way. Obviously they go to watch the games. We want skilful attacking football and we stress it all the time.

"That's exactly what we try to do. With my team last year we looked at bits of things from Barcelona and Argentina because we didn't have the tallest of teams so we thought we'd have to play a real combination type football. You try to play like the first team, but of course, that's determined by the players you've got. You try to do it but it evolves in the way that the players' natural abilities come out.

"For instance you now see a lot of the kids doing Ronaldo's trick where he chops the ball behind his leg while he's dribbling. A lot of the kids do that now because they watch him and try to emulate him and the other players. It's very infectious.

"We're lucky that we've got a great team to watch and a great history that makes you want to play that way. You've got to look at the best. You look at some clubs and it's pretty obvious they're just aiming to get their kids into the Championship or League One, no better than that, whereas I think you should be doing the best you can with them. Give them dreams. If you aim for the top and just miss, then you're still doing well, but if you're aiming three rungs down the ladder and miss, then you're nowhere."

Encouragement is the order of the day for United's youngsters. The traditional image of screaming, vein-bulging coaches kicking water bottles and berating their players is one the Carrington crew have made great efforts to steer clear from.

"One of the big things is that we try to get them to play with no fear, so we don't have anyone shouting at them from the sides," says McGuinness. "You see a lot of teams just telling the boys what to do all the time, and of course we'll talk to them and give them pointers, but we like to let them play during the game. That way there's no fear of being shouted at if you make a mistake."

7

STRENGTH IN RESERVE AND LOAN RANGERS

Logically, the outstanding talents of McGuinness' youth side are often fast-tracked up the development ladder and into United's Reserves. Formerly managed by Rene Meulensteen before his departure to Brondby, the second string were helmed by McClair and Jim Ryan throughout the 2006/07 campaign.

After garnering seven trophies in the previous two seasons, United's Reserves had to make do without any silverware at the end of the 2006/07 season. However, defeat in the final of the Manchester Senior

Brian McClair training with the Reserves.

Cup, coupled with finishing second in the Reserves league, was no mean feat given the scarcity of players at McClair and Ryan's disposal.

"We had a dirty dozen which was the core of the squad," admits McClair. "They did so well every day in training and in the games. We couldn't really afford any injuries and were often using boys from the U18s when they were available."

The shortage of dedicated Reserve team players is symptomatic of changes implemented by the Academy system in recent years. The abolition of U19s teams from the infrastructure has impacted upon the Reserve League, with clubs forced into fielding younger sides as a result.

"The Reserve League has changed dramatically in recent years," says Sir Alex Ferguson. "Once they got rid of the U19s, probably because of finance for other clubs, the Reserve team became really just a youth team.

"A lot of teams are just playing young lads, which created a problem for us, so now many of the really good young players are farmed out on loan. They need a bigger challenge than that. The Reserve team is still an important part of players' development, though."

Whereas the much-fabled Class of '92 largely made the step from Reserves to United's first team, young players at the club now see going out on loan as an extra rung on their development ladder. Recent seasons have seen a spate of United's youngsters temporarily plying their trade at other clubs across the globe.

With it becoming increasingly difficult to replicate high intensity competition, Sir Alex Ferguson and his Academy staff took the decision to crowbar loans into their players' development programme. Each move is tailor-made for each player, based on the coaching staff's assessment of what the individual needs to gain both on and off the pitch.

In the 2006/07 season alone, 15 players left United on loan at one stage or another, with some splitting their season between two temporary clubs. Giuseppe Rossi spent five months at Newcastle before joining Parma for the second half of their Serie A season, while Phil Bardsley had a similar arrangement at Rangers and Aston Villa.

A ready-made destination for United youngsters is Royal Antwerp, by virtue of the club's link-up with the Belgian side. Each year a handful of the Reds' best youngsters are sent over to Belgium to experience first team football, adapt to foreign culture and, of course, help

Sean Evans and Michael Lea do battle in training.

Antwerp in the pursuit of their ambitions.

"It's a great place for them to go for football and for lifetime skills," says Brian McClair. "Our ultimate dream would be that Antwerp become one of those top teams in Belgium and therefore are qualifying for European places, which would be of great benefit to our boys. We want players to play in the first team there, and come back with the great experience of European football, which they wouldn't have if they're loaned out to various places in England."

One man well aware of the benefits of the move to Belgium is John O'Shea. The Irish utility man spent a full season at Antwerp in his formative years, before going on to become an integral part of Sir Alex Ferguson's first team squad.

"It was huge for me," he says. "At the time the first team squad at

United was really big and obviously the team was doing so well. I'd been playing a lot in the Reserves, and I won't say it was getting easy for me, but it was comfortable.

"It wasn't as much of a challenge as it had been, and the manager felt that playing in the top league in Belgium would be a good test for me. Antwerp had just been promoted – [former Red] Luke Chadwick had played a big part in that – and playing in the top league was going to be difficult for them, because they were going to be underdogs each week.

"People back home in Ireland were saying I was finished at United because I'd been sent out to another team. The manager came to me and said, 'Look, this is just for your benefit, you'll be coming back', but obviously people away from the club don't see those things.

"It was a great test for me. My second game was at Anderlecht playing against [6' 7" Czech international striker] Jan Koller, which was a challenge! It was a great experience and I was learning a different culture and a different way of life. I matured a lot as a person as well.

"You see the benefits from the clubs who are getting the players too, especially looking at how well Sunderland did in 2006/7 with two of our lads [Jonny Evans and Danny Simpson]. It's a great chance because, as the manager says, the Reserves league has gone down a good few years in age – the average ages are down so much it's like a youth league now. The competitive action lads get through being at Antwerp, in the Championship, or elsewhere is fantastic experience and it's something the club can only benefit from."

The 2006/07 campaign saw United's relationship with Antwerp intensify, with Academy manager Brian McClair setting the challenge of gaining promotion back to the Belgian Premier League. One of the men entrusted with the smooth running of the link-up and the realisation of that ambition is former Leeds and Blackpool coach Andy Welsh, who joined United in 2006 and immediately assumed the role of assistant coach at Antwerp. A substantial part of his role is to look after United's loanees and integrate them into the Antwerp set-up.

"I thought it was an excellent project to get involved in," says Welsh. "It's a great experience for the boys both on and off the field, to play in front of big crowds and obviously our aim here is to get promotion. That's why I'm here."

The prospect of upping sticks and leaving behind the familiarity of friends, family and Carrington can be a daunting one for United's youngsters, but Welsh and his colleagues ensure that they are quickly integrated into the Antwerp way of life.

"They come out here and the accommodation we've got organised for them is great," he says. "Four of them live together in a very, very large five bedroom apartment which is huge for them. They all become part of the Antwerp squad, so obviously we've got to introduce them into a very eclectic squad. There are twelve different nationalities in the squad of about twenty-two players.

"With my experience I help and guide them both on and off the field. They have to do things like learn to drive on the opposite side of the road. We don't provide them with a chef so they have to organise the food. They have to eat the right food and learn to look after themselves a little bit more off the field. I take care of their training on the field so they're helped by [Antwerp manager] Warren Joyce and myself, and also by a lot of the other lads who have taken to our link-up excellently well.

"They go straight into the team and it's great for them to get first team experience in front of crowds. Last season had six games that were sell-outs of sixteen thousand and we don't get less than five thousand. The average home game is maybe around eight thousand, but derbies are always sell-outs and the players love that."

Somewhat inevitably, Welsh feels United's arrangement has prompted an undercurrent of envy in Belgian football towards Antwerp, who are seen in some quarters as being handed an unfair advantage.

"Obviously every club would love to link up with a club such as Manchester United," he says. "It's accepted, but obviously people look at it and are a little bit envious of it in certain ways. It goes well and I haven't really had any bad experiences of jealousy, but I would think there would be a few clubs who would consider it not to be a level playing field for Antwerp. They get the best four or five young players from one of the best clubs in the world to play for them for a season each year, so there's going to be a little bit of jealousy."

Such envy is of little concern to Antwerp's club secretary Paul Bistiaux, who delights in his side's link with United – not least because of the positive effects the Reds' youngsters have on Antwerp's performances.

"It is clear that many United players have had a big and sometimes decisive impact on our team over the years," says Bistiaux. "Danny Higginbotham, Ronnie Wallwork, Luke Chadwick, Kirk Hilton, John O'Shea, and more recently Dong Fangzhuo, Danny Simpson, Lee Martin and Adam Eckersley all made their mark and contributed hugely to our team's performance.

"Last season we enjoyed the presence of such talents as Jonny Evans, Fraizer Campbell, Darron Gibson and Ryan Shawcross. Put all these together and you have got a terrific team! Antwerp fans are proud of the association of their club with one of the biggest names in football and are happy with the link so far. They only wish sometimes that some of the United players could stay longer with our club, as they are often sorry to see them return to England after their loan spell."

Although Antwerp's staff and fans may harbour disappointment at the short nature of their relationship with the United players, the ultimate aim of the arrangement is to benefit the players themselves – something Welsh feels invariably occurs.

"Overall it's a success," he says. "For me I think all the lads we've had here have enjoyed it. Obviously it isn't Manchester United, and they don't have the same facilities they have at Carrington, me included, but it is good for them because it's first team football. That step between the Reserves and the first team at United is a massive, massive void to fill, but this sort of thing is a good first stage for them to fill that gap."

Danny Simpson and Jonny Evans both spent the first half of the 2006/07 season at Antwerp. The former was in his second spell in Belgium after finishing the previous campaign on loan with Welsh et al, giving him the unofficial title of tour guide for the uninitiated in his second stint.

"I knew what to expect," says Simpson. "I was going there with different lads and it was a different challenge starting the season all fresh and we knew the job we had to do. I was a bit more experienced, bringing Jonny, Fraizer [Campbell] and Darron [Gibson].

"You go from U18s to Reserves and then the next step is Antwerp. There are maybe ten thousand fans watching every week, you're in a different country and you're on your own looking after yourselves. I enjoyed it, we had a good run in the first half of the season before I left."

"It was a great experience for me and the other lads who were over there at the time," adds Evans. "It's been a real stepping stone and a great benefit for our career."

So superior was Evans' form that he incredibly became a full Northern Ireland international while on loan at Antwerp. His superb displays on the international scene forced him into the spotlight, and it was no surprise when he spent the second half of his season on loan at ambitious Championship side Sunderland under the management of United legend Roy Keane.

The former Reds skipper also recruited Simpson on loan until the end of the campaign, and both players swiftly became integral parts of the Black Cats' amazing league run which saw one defeat in 19 games, and ended with promotion to the Premiership.

"I moved onto Sunderland and the season just went really well," admits the Salford-born defender. "At big clubs like United and Sunderland everyone expects you to win every game. Your performances have got to be at a high standard, and me and Jonny tried to maintain that.

"It was a very good experience. I think I improved under Roy Keane and playing with those players and training with them every day. I was really pleased with how it went up there and it was a good step for me."

For Evans, the most eye-opening aspect of being catapulted from Reserve team football to the high stakes of the Championship via the Belgian second division is the pressure of playing in front of passionate fans.

"Antwerp are a big club in Belgium, they possibly have as big a stature over there as Sunderland have in the North East, with very passionate fans always expecting the best, and that's what's expected at Sunderland too," he says. "I think what helps when you're younger is not to make mistakes, I think that's a big part of it because if you make mistakes at that level then the fans could be on your back as quick as they've grown to like you."

While Evans and Simpson benefited hugely from their loan deals, even their success pales in comparison to that of goalkeeper Ben Foster. Immediately after joining United in July 2005, Foster spent the entire 2005/06 and 2006/07 seasons on loan at Watford, with dramatic results. The former Stoke City stopper was one of the main inspirations in the Hornets' unlikely promotion from the Championship to the Premier League in his first season, and he ended up on the standby list for England's 2006 World Cup squad.

His meteoric rise continued throughout his second season there where, in a brighter spotlight, he garnered plaudits aplenty for his superb displays for Aidy Boothroyd's side and won his first England cap, against Spain at Old Trafford.

Although Foster's domestic heroics couldn't prevent the Hornets from returning to the Championship, he has no doubt about the benefits of his two seasons at Vicarage Road compared to the alternative of warming the bench at United.

"It benefited me massively," he says. "It just got me on to bigger and bigger things really. Obviously, being in the England squad and making my debut came from my exposure in the Premiership with Watford. It wasn't just the exposure though, I think my game was brought on so much during my time there. The goalkeeping coach Alec Chamberlain did a lot of work with me and brought me on a lot, and obviously playing week in, week out was everything that a young goalie like me

Jonny Evans in action against Shenzhen FC during United's pre-season tour to the Far East in July 2007.

dreams of. It's a move which just did everything for me really.

"Obviously there's no way I would have been in the England squad if I'd been playing for United's Reserves for two seasons. All a young goal-keeper needs really is experience, and playing in front of big crowds helps as well. When you're playing Reserves football, in the back of your head it doesn't really matter so much, you can make a mistake and it's not really the end of the world. There are not thousands and thousands of people watching you, a football club's livelihood isn't at stake.

"Then take my first season at Watford, the last game was the play-off final. There was around eighty thousand people watching inside the ground with forty million pounds riding on the game – that's the pressure that you're talking about and you certainly don't get that in Reserves football."

8

THE RECRUITMENT PROCESS

While the sales-driven British media were busy linking United with a raft of big-name outfield signings in the summer of 2005, the arrival of Ben Foster barely registered a jot on the transfer seismograph. The England goalkeeper came into United's clutches through painstaking research from Sir Alex Ferguson's scouting team – although good fortune did play a part in Foster initially coming to the club's attention.

The United manager was in the Millennium Stadium crowd to watch

Ben Foster, United's surprise signing in summer 2005, is seen here on tour in Soweto the following year.

his son Darren, then of Wrexham, in the Football League Trophy final against Southend in April 2005. Although Darren notched the trophy-clinching second goal in a 2-0 win, it was Foster – then on loan with the Welsh side – who caught Sir Alex's eye.

"I remember during the game looking up at the big screen and seeing the camera pan down on to Sir Alex Ferguson," recalls Foster. "I remember thinking 'Oh right, he's here today', and of course it didn't cross my mind that he could end up being interested in signing me. But that's when he saw me, and then I think he asked Darren a bit about me and it went from there. I played quite well and then for the remaining games of the season he sent Tony Coton to come and watch me."

The pursuit of Foster was, in fact, a relatively short one. The arrivals of Ji-sung Park, Anderson and Nani, for instance, came after each player was evaluated from the stands on countless occasions by one or more members of United's scouting team.

Chief scout Jim Lawlor heads up the unit dedicated to running the rule over forthcoming opponents and potential signings, and it has scouts located in countries across the globe, in places as diverse as Salford and Santiago.

"We have one of the bigger scouting networks because we look to recruit the very best players in the world and you can't do that by scouting in just one country," says Lawlor. "We have an extensive network which is growing all the time. Hopefully, that will help us acquire the very best players.

"We have our greatest number of scouts in the UK. But players can come from anywhere in the world. You only have to look at some of the top players in world football and they come from small countries in Africa and other places. So we keep our scouts active everywhere and keep an open mind."

There are no hard and fast rules regarding how signings arrive at United. Some, such as Ole Gunnar Solskjaer, Nani, Anderson or Park are shock newcomers, largely unknown outside the countries in which they ply their trades, and arrive with little media fanfare. Others, like Wayne Rooney and Owen Hargreaves, come at the end of high-profile, protracted chases.

The plan Lawlor and his team endeavour to stick to, however, is one of finding the perfect player to fill existing or looming vacancies within Sir Alex Ferguson's squad.

"We look at the squad and examine where we have strengths and weaknesses and players with injuries," says Lawlor. "We make priorities based on that. But anyone who's of the quality we need in any position will always attract interest. Our scouting network can throw up players in all positions, at any time of the year. But the scouts do have priorities both in the January window and in the summer.

"We have long-term planning in relation to different positions. Sometimes we bring in young players who we're looking to develop over a number of years, and other times we are looking to fill positions immediately and we need a player to come in and do a job in the first team straight away."

The inflated cost of shopping for English talent has not been lost on United. As shown by the 2004 arrivals of Italian striker Giuseppe Rossi and Spanish defender Gerard Pique from Parma and Barcelona respectively, United's scouts cast a wide net for all age groups in the modern era.

"Scouting has changed," says Sir Alex. "We scout abroad more than we have ever done and particularly for good talent. That part has changed, but the essential part, i.e. players for the first team, never changes. We try to get what we need."

When the scouts have made their recommendations, Sir Alex often casts his own eye over the target in action before sanctioning a bid for the player.

"Sometimes I go to games just to give another opinion on a player, I've always done that," he says. "Sometimes I don't need to make a personal check on a player because they're an obvious target, like Wayne Rooney for example."

If the manager likes what he sees, then he puts a request in to chief executive David Gill, who specialises in – and thrives on – the thrill of the chase for new arrivals. Over to you, David.

"Signing a player is all about tactics," admits Gill. "Alex will come to me when he's identified a player he wants to sign and it's then up to me to go away and start negotiations."

The Glazer family takeover of United inherently gives them the definitive yay-or-nay on any new signings, but it is Gill who still conducts negotiations with players and agents in such situations.

"Obviously I keep the Glazers informed of our plans and receive their ultimate approval for the expenditure," he says before adding, with a smile, "I get a lot of satisfaction when I see the player sign on the dotted line."

Part Three

OLD TRAFFORD DAY-TO-DAY

"Sir Matt Busby had the original idea about introducing corporate boxes and developing United into a successful business as well as a football club. He always had a vision of where the club was going and how it would end up, and I think the current set-up is pretty much what he would have envisaged." **SIR BOBBY CHARLTON**

9

BOARD GAMES

F ew could have predicted the impact two wily Scots would have on the history and ongoing success on and off the pitch at Old Trafford. In the Reds' two managerial knights – Sir Matt Busby and Sir Alex Ferguson – the club have been blessed by a pair of football visionaries who have blazed their own trails both on and away from the football field. The late Sir Matt, who sadly passed away in January 1994, dragged United and his remaining Busby Babes up from the depths of despair in the wake of the Munich air disaster in 1958, leading them to European glory just ten years later on that balmy night at Wembley when the Reds crushed a Eusebio-inspired Benfica side 4-1 after extra time.

Sir Matt Busby's influence on United lives on to this day.

Club directors Bryan, Abi and Joel Glazer share a joke at Old Trafford.

Sir Alex would later emulate his former mentor, fittingly on the night that Matt would have celebrated his 90th birthday on 26 May 1999. Many believe he was looking down on his beloved Reds that night – how else could one explain that freakish final three minutes when United came from a goal down in injury time to claim the club's second European Cup triumph – and a Treble to boot – against all the odds? Divine intervention it surely was.

Such success on the pitch has seen the club grow into just as big a force off it. No longer is Manchester United simply a football club, albeit the biggest in the world at that, it is an inimitable business empire leading the way in countless fields, from media to marketing, sponsorship to hospitality. And, of course, it boasts the biggest club stadium in the UK with a sell-out 76,000 capacity every week.

The man entrusted with the smooth running of the business side of things is chief executive and United fan David Gill. Since joining the club, initially as finance director, in 1997, Gill, who took over the power reins from Peter Kenyon in September 2003, has been instrumental in the club's commercial evolution over the last 20 years on the back of the team's domestic domination during the 1990s. Despite the furore around the Glazer family taking over United in 2005, Gill insists that little has changed, and the club remains in good shape.

"In general I think things have settled down since the takeover," he insists. "There was clearly some turmoil prior to it happening because change is always something you have to think about. But I spent time with the family and got to understand what they are all about, and they have been true to their word. They said they wouldn't change things in terms of how the club is run, either by Alex on the football side, or by myself on the non-football side, and that has been the case. They have been there when we've needed them, both in finding money for new players and for improving the contracts of current ones, but also in an equally constructive way with various sponsorship deals. It's an area in which they feel they can add value and they were instrumental in securing our record-breaking shirt deal with AIG [in April 2006].

"There will always be a minority of fans who are opposed to the situation, but the fans can't complain about too much given how well the team have been doing. Football clubs are special places, and the Glazer family understand stability is a key requirement in any sports team if you are to have success on the pitch."

Weekly conversations with Gill ensure the family, who also own American football outfit Tampa Bay Buccaneers, are kept firmly abreast of events at Old Trafford. Gill insists their investment in the club is part of a long-term strategy that will allow the club to grow as a business.

"They see this as a long-term project," says Gill. "You only need to look at their investment philosophy, whether it's at the Buccaneers or at United, they invest for the long term. They see the growth in football and they want to be a part of it.

"They follow what's happening at the club very closely. They watch every game on television and come over to matches at Old Trafford when they can. I also make three or four business trips to America to see them each year. I have a scheduled conference call with Joel and two or three of the other brothers every week which can last anywhere between half an hour to an hour depending on the issues we need to discuss. Aside from that I speak to Joel about certain issues as they arise. If there is a particular matter regarding a player or a possible transfer, I'll give him a call. We ensure that we're both available at any time, day or night."

United's record-breaking £56.5 million shirt deal with AIG – one of the world's biggest companies that specialises in insurance and financial services – has opened significant doors to both the Far East and the American markets. Forming links with such organisations continues to be of prime importance for the Reds' worldwide business plan.

"Deals like the ones we have with AIG and Nike are very important in helping to expand United's global profile," explains Gill. "Our job is to develop and improve the revenues of the club, which we can then invest back into the team, whether it is through buying new players, renewing current players' contracts, or developing aspects of Carrington and Old Trafford. We have to keep pushing the whole club, including the business side, further forward. We have a worldwide coverage and that helps us to attract investors.

"Our deal with AIG was a particularly interesting one because it was sold at a time when the team weren't firing on all cylinders. We were out of the Champions League and the FA Cup and also struggling in the Premiership. But we still managed to sell that deal to one of the biggest companies in the world. That shows the pulling power of Manchester United and the resonance of our name on a global basis."

Nevertheless, Gill insists the football side of the club will always be paramount to United's commercial aspirations.

"We have never strayed from the whole ethos that the football is the most critical thing," he insists. "We support Alex and the players in any way we can and will invest whatever funds we feel we need to in order to give the team on the pitch the best possible chance of success. But in order to do that we have to do deals and look at different areas of the business. Some things work, others don't. But we're always looking at ways we can expand the business because that will inevitably have an effect on what happens on the pitch."

An average day for Gill usually constitutes a 12-hour shift. One of the first to arrive at Old Trafford just after 7 a.m., he heads straight to his office, within the inner sanctums of the stadium's East Stand, to prepare for the day ahead. With just over 450 members of staff spread across 25 different departments (situated at both Old Trafford and Carrington) to manage, life is never dull for United's chief commander.

"No day is ever the same," says David. "I always have a quick look at

Owen Hargreaves is welcomed to United by David Gill on 27 June 2007 – the summer is always a hectic time for the Reds' chief executive.

Sir Alex and David Gill have a great working relationship: 'We both want the same thing, which is success for Manchester United on and off the pitch.'

the papers as soon as I get into the office. Di Law [football media manager] checks through them thoroughly and sends me a note on anything that's relevant to United. I'll have a look at it and give her a response if I feel I need to, so she can deal with the media as necessary. The majority of my day is usually taken up by internal and external meetings, telephone calls and answering emails. I'll often have other matters to deal with, such as those relating to my role on the FA Board, or G14 matters. I might make a couple of calls about players we're interested in signing and may also deal with a number of other matters around the club.

"During the transfer windows, particularly the summer one, my time is much more focused on player activity – trying to secure possible transfers and finalising details around players' contracts. The variety of the job is something I enjoy. There are tedious aspects to it, but the buzz you get from signing a player you've coveted for a long time or seeing the team win a trophy is fantastic – I get as much satisfaction by what we achieve off the field, as well as on it.

"We have wonderful and loyal staff at the club, the vast majority of whom worship the place and it is a privilege to work with them. I usually leave the office between six and seven in the evening and tend to turn my Blackberry off when I get home. If someone like Alex really needs to speak to me he'll just call me at home."

Gill's relationship with the United boss is central to the smooth amalgamation of the football and commercial aspects of the club. And it's one that continues to prove fruitful.

"Alex and I work very well together and respect each other very much," says Gill. "We talk most days and I have a meeting with him at Carrington once a week. He's clearly a very single-minded character but we both want the same thing, which is success for Manchester United on and off the pitch, and we're both driven by that goal.

"Alex's achievements with the club have been amazing. He works extremely hard and certainly puts the hours in. In my experience most people who are at the top of the tree in their profession are the type of personalities who are never satisfied. They always crave more and are continually looking forward. If you ally that with their skills, you've got a great combination, and that's often what sets them apart. Success in sport is very difficult to sustain, but Alex has managed to do that. His ability to make difficult decisions is legendary. He recognises that it's part of the job. He's always understood what United means in terms of the club's football style and he has always delivered that. We want to win, but we want to win in the United way."

The players themselves are well aware of the history and traditions that engulf daily life at Old Trafford and they are the type of traits that are seemingly impossible to turn down when it comes to attracting new players.

"There were a few teams interested in signing me, but once I knew United had been in contact I made it clear it was the only place I wanted to go," recalls Wayne Rooney, who joined in the summer of 2004 from Everton. "After watching them win everything and play brilliant football all through the nineties, I wanted to be a part of the club. The way United play attacking football is brilliant and they were the one team that most suited the way I play. I want to win medals in my career and there's nowhere better to do that than here."

"Being at United is like living a dream," adds Darren Fletcher. "It's a cliché, but to be able to get up every morning and train at Carrington before a match at Old Trafford on a Saturday is unbelievable and an absolute honour. I can't believe it's my job. Playing for a club like United, which is always challenging for the top honours, is a real privilege."

At times during the season the players are required to make special appearances at sponsorship and marketing events, while photo-shoots or filming around United-supported projects are also part of life as a Manchester United footballer. Finding an optimum balance between activities on and off the pitch can prove a delicate juggling act, but John O'Shea reckons the Reds have things spot on.

"United is such a massive institution but it's still a family club, which makes it a very special place to be," insists the Irish international. "The success we've had on the pitch has made it into one of the biggest clubs in the world commercially and financially, but I think the club have found a very good balance with things on the football side and outside the game, and I think that will continue to go from strength to strength."

One man who has witnessed the club's spiralling development over the last 50-plus years is Reds' legend and club director Sir Bobby Charlton. A Busby Babe under Sir Matt, Charlton skippered United to their European triumph in 1968 having picked up a World Cup winners' medal two years earlier. An iconic figure of the club's history, Sir Bobby still spends much of his time in and around the club and is clearly content with the current set-up under the Glazer family.

"There has been no reason at all to criticise the owners for interfering or anything like that," he reasons. "They've let everyone here get on with their jobs as they've always done. Yes they own the biggest club in the world, but they haven't really made massive changes, which has allowed everyone to get on with things.

"As well as being a football club, Manchester United is now an enormous business. The facilities are unbelievable. There are so many different departments nowadays, from catering to merchandising to media. All of them play a big part in helping to produce the money that we need to keep a place this size going."

Sir Bobby's ambassadorial role at the club is one that takes him all over the world. He marvels at United's global appeal and believes the club's ever-increasing profile and stature, both at home and abroad, is something that his former manager would be extremely proud of.

"Matt Busby had the original idea about introducing corporate boxes and developing the club into a successful business as well as a football club," reveals Sir Bobby. "He felt that if United were going to become one of the biggest clubs in the world, then we would actually have to get out there and get the finance. Matt always had a vision of where this place was going and how it would end up. Alex came along and carried that vision through, and I think the current set-up is pretty much what Matt would have envisaged. But we must always look forward. As a club we're never afraid to take chances and we must work hard to maintain our high standards. We can never stand still."

Standing still is not something Rio Ferdinand believes he will ever see at Old Trafford.

"This club is an ever-evolving place," he declares. "It's almost like there are revolving doors because the personnel on the pitch is constantly changing. That has always been the case and that will continue to be the case because high standards have got to be kept. If people aren't hitting those standards the manager will see it and he'll bring in new players and get people who aren't producing out of the door.

"When I joined United the likes of Becks [David Beckham], Ruud

Sir Bobby Charlton talks to UEFA president Michel Platini ahead of the friendly against a Europe XI on 13 March 2007.

van Nistelrooy, Roy Keane and Seba Veron were all here. They were four great players and at the time you couldn't see United doing without them. You thought they'd be here for the rest of their careers. But as is the case in football, things change. I certainly believe the current team can do well in the coming seasons. The important thing to remember is, it's all about sustaining that success."

Maintaining a high level of success away from the match action is what David Gill in particular is continuing to strive for, and the chief executive believes there are great prospects in store for the Reds over the coming years.

"The game continues to grow and I think there are plenty of opportunities for us," he says confidently. "The challenge in any business is to continue to produce a great product, and ours is out on the pitch. Winning football matches in the Manchester United way is what we want to see. One of the major challenges in the future will be finding a replacement for Alex when he eventually decides to call it a day – that'll be a critical time for the club.

"There are always things to get your teeth into whether it is players' contracts, dealing with the media or negotiating new commercial deals. The club possesses some great assets, like the stadium, and we now have stable ownership which we didn't have in the final years as a quoted PLC. Overall, I think the future looks very bright and I think we need to stay positive going forward. I feel very optimistic about everything."

Much of that optimism can be attributed to the unique leadership skills and vision of two great Scots who, according to 1968 European Cup winner and MUTV pundit Paddy Crerand, may one day be standing side by side once more at Old Trafford.

"It's amazing to think how much both Matt and Alex have done for this club," says Paddy. "In the future I'm sure there will be a statue of the pair of them stood together outside the stadium."

What a fitting image that would be.

IN THE PUBLIC EYE

10

"**D**on't always believe what you read in the papers" goes the saying and it's one that could not ring any truer than at Old Trafford. Pick up any one of the daily red tops, or broadsheets for that matter, and you're virtually guaranteed to find a story on United both in season and out. Such is the voracious appetite for news about the Reds that the media spotlight that shines so strongly over Old Trafford throughout the season rarely diminishes over the summer months. In fact, you could argue it burns even brighter during the silly season that is the transfer window.

"When I first joined the club [in 1997] the spotlight on United was

Rio Ferdinand and John O'Shea cast an eye over some of the tabloid press.

Ryan Giggs gives an impromptu interview to the press.

huge, but now it's even greater," insists chief executive David Gill. "You have to be fairly thick skinned about some things because a lot of false information ends up in the media. The world is such a small place nowadays because of the huge press coverage on the internet and satellite television which broadcasts twenty-four/seven. I certainly can't see the interest in the game abating. It was big both as a sport and as a business at the time I joined United but it's got even bigger since we moved into the twenty-first century. Given that we're one of the world's top clubs, we'll undoubtedly continue to get more than our fair share of media coverage. That's not something we'll complain about though because if we weren't being covered it would mean that we weren't top of the tree."

The man entrusted with managing what United feed to the insatiable tabloid hacks is communications director Phil Townsend. Aided by Carrington-based football media manager Diana Law, who keeps Sir Alex Ferguson firmly up to date on the United stories making the headlines, and communications officer Karen Shotbolt, Phil fields calls and emails from news hungry journalists on the hunt for a back-page scoop on a daily basis. United have a strict policy of not commenting on transfer speculation, while close consultation with David Gill and, if required the club's owners, will be carried out before any official statements are released. But, according to Phil, even that doesn't always suffice.

"There is an insatiable appetite for news about Manchester United and I don't think that's something we'll ever be able to fulfil," he concedes. "People are always interested in whatever we do. I think we are a little more aware than we used to be of the pressure that journalists are under from their editors to produce stories about the club. We try very hard to behave in a manner which is in the best interests of the club, while attempting to meet the journalists' needs as much as we can. But at the same time we genuinely don't believe that there is enough material to satisfy that demand on a daily basis.

"The Manchester United where I work is very different to the Manchester United that people think exists. The great thing about this club is we operate right at the centre of a whole whirlwind of noise and colour, but actually on many occasions this is the calmest place you can be. Sometimes coming in to work can be the best way to get away from outside opinions."

The intensity of today's media is such that you're either top of the tree or in perpetual crisis. The latter scenario is one that some blood-thirsty scribes love to thrust upon United in the aftermath of a defeat, but Townsend, who joined the club in February 2004, insists United have grown a thick enough skin to cope with the flack.

"I believe we have a mature attitude to criticism, which is helpful," says Phil, who is on call 24/7 and even had to work on Christmas Day when the club announced the signing of Nemanja Vidic back in 2005. "We don't rush into responding to everything written about us. Despite what our private views might be, it is sometimes not worth dignifying an accusation with a response. We have an ability to draw a line and only get drawn in when the line is crossed. We recognise that there is value in being in the papers as a high profile club. We don't always like what is written, but the fact that we are so widely discussed enables us to persuade potential investors that we're a company worth backing because of our global reach.

"My predecessor Paddy Harveson [now the Prince of Wales' communications secretary] always said to me that if the team are doing well, the number of calls you get tends to drop off," he adds. "It's fair to say there are fewer incidences of crisis management when set against a backdrop of a winning team. In recent years we've also stepped up internal communications and have made a point of trying to improve our links with supporters. On the whole, I think we're pretty responsive to all situations."

Given the wide array of stories written and spoken about United it's inevitable that some of those produced simply beggar belief.

"I've certainly read some bizarre things about the club over the years," smiles Phil, who is based in Old Trafford's East Stand. "We have not, for example, developed a machine for rotating footballs so that players can sign them for charity. Nor have we put microchips under the players' skin to keep tabs on their social lives!"

United's current position as a private company means the Reds now have a much tighter control over their PR stance.

"Things on the communication side have changed since the Glazer family took over because we are no longer governed by stringent stock market rules like we were during the PLC days," explains Townsend. "The debate over whether or not we comment on certain stories was more of an issue when we were a PLC because a negative or false story in the press could have affected the share price.

"Not having to worry about regulatory announcements at seven in the morning or trying to make sure we stabilise the share price has made things much easier. The unveiling of our record-breaking shirt deal with AIG for example was a much simpler process because we were able to keep everything in-house. We're now much more in control of what we can proactively announce, which allows us to create some element of surprise on occasion."

The element of surprise is something that Sir Alex Ferguson has sprung on many a tabloid hack over the years and indeed used to his advantage as part of his famous mind games with opposition managers. But even he despairs at the media industry and the sensationalism that seems to engulf it.

"Today's media is a different kind from when I started as a young manager," insists the Boss, who comes face-to-face with the British media at his weekly Friday press conference at Carrington. "It's very competitive. They [the journalists] are all under pressure, every one of them, so you therefore get so much sensationalism and also so many false stories. They cut so many corners dramatically now. It's not an easy profession, I understand that, but even so it's not easy for us to accept it. I don't read much of the papers at all and I don't look forward to the press conferences, but I've got to do them, there's nothing else for it."

Former MUTV chief commentator Steve Bower, who still has an excellent relationship with the gaffer, says timing and judgement is crucial during interview situations with Sir Alex.

"You learn subconsciously when to ask things, when not to ask things and also when to wrap things up, just by his body language or even his eyes," explains Steve, who now works for Setanta Sports. "The hardest time to interview the manager is after a game, because emotions are running high. Sometimes, like when United went out of the FA Cup to Liverpool in February 2006 or when Thierry Henry scored an injury-time winner during United's game at Arsenal [in January 2007], the last thing he wants is a microphone shoved in his face, but you have to

ask the questions. Those are the hardest interviews. In fairness to him though, he's always been very, very good with me."

According to Press Association chief football writer Simon Stone, another one of the select few tasked with tracking everyday events at the world's biggest club, the Reds' boss enjoys rare respect and reverence among the press hordes which few are afforded.

"Having been manager of United for over twenty years now, Sir Alex has done it all as far as the media is concerned," concedes Stone. "At this stage of his career, he appears far more relaxed than he used to be, although that doesn't stop him pointing out, in fairly forceful terms, if he believes a reporter has either overstepped the mark or got something wrong. No one is immune from such tongue-lashings but some suffer more than others. Nevertheless, because of his enormous success he is greatly respected by everyone in the media."

Sir Alex's view of a press conference – he knows the level of media interest in United is never going to wane.

Stone, who also covers the England team home and abroad, says life is never dull as a Manchester United correspondent and admits there is a fine balancing act between keeping peace with the club while trying to avoid a reprimand from an angry editor for failing to break a United exclusive.

"Some journalists do not even attempt to try and navigate the situation," admits Stone. "But ultimately all reporters are paid by their newspapers not the club, so the loyalty must be getting news into print. Manchester United enjoys such worldwide support that virtually everything that happens around the club is of major interest. Everyone has an opinion on them, good or bad. Other clubs attract big crowds, win trophies and spend lots of money, but none comes close to United. The desire for news from Old Trafford is therefore insatiable and the competition to be the first to break it is huge. All reporters stand or fall by the stories they get and because so many people are interested in United, any little snippet can be back page news, allowing the journalists to justify themselves to their demanding sports editors. As a reporter, there is nothing that gives you the kind of buzz you get from breaking a big story."

Stone says the advent of official club websites and sophisticated public relations departments has made netting a scoop on the Reds a much tougher exercise than it once was.

"It's the same at every major club nowadays," explains Stone, who was one of the first to reveal that Roy Keane was quitting Old Trafford back in November 2005. "Clubs hold more control over their news than they have ever done and, understandably, try to ensure all stories present their respective clubs in the best light possible. Clearly, it is not possible to control everything and the biggest-selling regional, daily and Sunday newspapers compete fiercely for the most interesting pieces of information.

"When you take into account the huge footballing figures associated with United – Sir Alex Ferguson, Wayne Rooney and Cristiano Ronaldo to name but three, it is little wonder fans are so keen to know what is going on. Sometimes the stories are true, sometimes they are not. But undoubtedly more words are written about United than any other club."

Such is the attention heaped on modern-day footballers, particularly those in English football's top flight, that photo-shoots and personal appearances are now par for the course. Some enjoy it, others don't, but the off-the-field activities show no signs of abating.

Perfecting their poses for the cameras is an exercise the players are required to do at the club's highly anticipated photo-shoot for the launch of a new kit.

The team's ensemble for the 2007/08 season comprises an all-red shirt with a stylish white stripe running down the back of the jersey featuring a mini devil and it's a popular choice among the team. The all-black away kit with its neat red trim also seems to go down well with the players who are aptly suited and booted for the occasion.

"These kinds of things are what you have to do as a Manchester United player," says club skipper Gary Neville. "It's important that our fans throughout the world see us in our new kit and for that reason we have to do these photo-shoots. We always have a good laugh and take the mickey out of the photographers!"

Designing a new kit is an 18-month process, the first part of which involves United providing a brief to Nike, the club's official sportswear partner. They in turn will present a paper version of the initial design to chief executive David Gill and marketing relationship director Luisa D'Aprano who then feed their comments back to Nike and the Glazer family.

"Once we feel the look, feel and direction of the shirt is right, we'll then sit down with Sir Alex so he can give his input," explains Luisa. "The kit design is not something the players get involved in but the manager always has a say in terms of the design and also the fabric. It's important that he, David Gill and the club owners are all comfortable with it and feel it's right because it's the club shirt – it's such a prominent part of what United is all about."

The club's partnership with leading sports giants Nike has proved a fruitful one for both parties. Signed in 2002, the 13-year deal continues to go from strength to strength.

"Nike's long-term partnership with United is a great asset to the club," continues Luisa. "The events that they do around merchandising and Manchester United Soccer Schools gives them the ability to reach out to people globally which in turn benefits us; certain aspects of what they do dovetail into what we do. We work really closely with them and the overall partnership is a very productive and profitable one for both companies."

"I enjoy the media side sometimes," admits Wayne Rooney. "Obviously when you're young you watch football and that's all you're interested in. But once you start playing you realise that the other stuff is part of your job as well. You've got to do off-the-field stuff even if you don't want to, I appreciate that and I try to do it the best that I can."

United receive numerous requests from all over the world for time with individual players every week. In the main these applications stem from club media and rights' holders such as the BBC and Sky TV, but there is also a seemingly endless trail of additional requests from other external media organisations from places as far flung as Asia. And as Rio Ferdinand explains they are not always what they seem.

"I've been asked to pose naked a few times but I don't think my mum would be too pleased if I did that!" he smiles. "I once turned up for a photo-shoot and had to sit among a hundred rabbits! It was horrible. I'm not an animal lover at all and they were doing their business every-where during the shoot! It wasn't a nice experience.

"The massive spotlight on this club is something that's always been there," he adds. "I remember Nicky Butt saying to me before I signed that when you become a United player you're not just joining a football club, you're joining an institution. People live and breathe this club, it's their life. You only really realise how big it is when you arrive. I said the same thing to Michael Carrick before he signed. It's just phenomenal."

United's own media assets, including the award-winning official website (which attracts well over three million unique visitors per month), a monthly magazine and matchday programme, which are fed by one editorial team from Haymarket Media Group, as well as in-house television channel MUTV, and the Reds' exclusive book deal with Orion Publishing, represent an integral part of the club's internal business structure. Chief executive David Gill says they will continue to be a crucial element of the club's plans.

"The bulk of our media income comes from the collective television deals around the Premiership and Champions League, but we also make money from other media assets such as the website and MUTV," explains Gill. "The fact that we have our own media business sets us apart from other clubs. What we'd like to do, as we've done with the Haymarket deal, is to have more of an integrated approach and bring everything under one roof. We're looking at plans for the creation of a designated media centre in the future.

"The media has changed immeasurably over the last ten years and it'll change again over the next decade. We need to understand what's happening in the technological world and make sure we're aware of issues that will affect our business. We must also ensure we have as much ownership of the club's media assets as we possibly can, while retaining as much flexibility as we can, whereby we're not held back by a contract of some sort which prevents us from getting involved in certain projects. The media is certainly a critical element for us."

The Reds' director of media, Sameer Pabari, says providing up-to-date and accurate information to the fans via the club's various media outlets is United's primary aim.

"Our operations are very broad and it's actually quite rare for a business to participate in so many different media channels," he explains. "Of course, it's a business, but it's also a service for our supporters. The website in particular is essentially part of the very infrastructure of the club and it's the way in which many fans, both in the UK and worldwide, interact with United.

"MUTV is another important element of the structure. It was set up in 1998, from which point it has grown substantially both in terms of its size and its subscription figures and it is now broadcast in around forty countries.

"Aside from the print and broadcast side, we have a mobile business, MU Mobile, and we've also set up a deal to distribute photographic images owned by the club in conjunction with Getty Images, one of the largest photographic agencies in the world. In addition to that, we also have certain media rights which we grant to external parties such as radio rights which are currently utilised by the BBC and Xfm. It's my role to manage all of these different activities and to work with our partners to create the best media products we can."

Trying to stay one step ahead of the rest is crucial to future success and Sameer is confident the Reds can maintain their high level of productivity and quality.

It's a family affair for MUTV presenter Hayley McQueen and her father, ex-Red Gordon.

"As a business, we need to move with the times and that's something we're working on," he adds. "The way in which we have brought the print side under one umbrella is an example of that. We now have one editorial team feeding the website, the matchday programme and the magazine in a much more consistent and coherent manner and that's something we want to look at in terms of the audio visual side as well. We want to continue to produce high-quality material and rather than just looking at other football clubs, I think we need to start comparing ourselves with market-leading media organisations. That needs to be our benchmark."

With an ever-growing portfolio of media assets, United continue to set the off-the-field benchmark for the rest of the football world.

11

LAYING THE FOUNDATIONS

Though not always publicised, Sir Alex Ferguson and his players lend a big chunk of their time and support to a number of community and charity campaigns, via the Manchester United Foundation.

The Foundation was launched in June 2006 as part of the celebrations to mark the 50th anniversary of the Busby Babes' first league title. Designed to use the power of football and the Manchester United name as a motivational tool, it has a clear vision to educate, motivate and inspire

Ryan Giggs with just one of the beneficiaries of the Manchester United Foundation.

Cristiano Ronaldo takes on Gennaro Gattuso and Roberto Ayala during the March 2007 friendly against a Europe XI, which raised more than £1.3 million for the Foundation.

future generations to build better communities for all in the Northwest and around the world. The Foundation is a registered charity and also operates a trading company which raises funds to fulfil its objectives.

Managed by a board of trustees which is comprised of current players, including club captain Gary Neville, ex-players such as Denis Irwin, and a number of internal and external figures, the Foundation runs a number of different programmes via various departments which now fall under its broad remit. These cut across a range of diverse levels, including the schools football programme, girls' football and the disability football programme, to education, which includes link-ups with the club's Study Support Centre, and outside organisations, such as The Prince's Trust and Premier League Reading Stars, to the partner-ship with global children's charity UNICEF. The trading company operates the lotteries (formerly known as MUDA) and also manages the relationship with United's preferred charity partners on behalf of the club. In the summer of 2007, the Foundation also appointed two national charity partners – the Cystic Fibrosis Trust and the Children's Society – and four local partners – Francis House Children's Hospice, the New Children's Hospital Appeal, Rainbow House and Christie's Hospital – for a period of three years. Through these partnerships, the Foundation aims to raise £2 million for a range of identified projects which will make a major difference to children and young people in the Northwest and around the country.

With a 12-month programme of events already planned, the Foundation hopes to channel the worldwide passion for United to influence positive change within communities.

"We haven't just got a moral obligation to help out local communities, we also have a real wish to do so," says Communications Director Phil Townsend. "Historically, our community departments have been run as individual operations, but now they're under one umbrella we have an excellent platform from which to significantly expand the set-up.

"The Foundation is an ambassador of Manchester United and we're looking to increase income by developing relationships with commercial partners. We hope that by 2012 the Foundation will have a turnover of around three to four million pounds. The more money we have, the greater impact we can have on our communities."

The first major event organised by the Foundation was the UEFA charity match at Old Trafford in March 2007 which saw United come face-to-face with an all-star European XI managed by Italian World Cup-winning manager Marcello Lippi. The one-off game marked two jubilees: United's half-century of involvement in European competitions, and the 50th anniversary of the Treaty of Rome, which laid the foundations for a united Europe. A sell-out crowd of over 74,000 watched the action unfold and also witnessed a special half-time appearance by former Red David Beckham, who made an emotional speech to the fans he had been unable to say goodbye to following his highly publicised switch to Real Madrid in the summer of 2003.

Club secretary Ken Ramsden played an integral role in the organisation of the historic event, which he believes summed up the very essence of Manchester United.

"To get more than seventy-four thousand people through the

turnstiles on a winter's night for a friendly match in the middle of a busy season tells you all you'll ever need to know about this club," he explains. "Nobody else in the world could ever, ever do that and it was another good example of the uniqueness of this place.

"It was tremendously demanding to coordinate, but at the end of the day, it was a fantastic and entertaining occasion for everyone. It was an event that Manchester United specialises in and the response we received was phenomenal."

The match, which ended 4-3 to United, raised in excess of £1.3 million, which will be invested into a number of future projects over the next decade and beyond.

"It was a fantastic event and one that generated both interest and money far beyond our expectations," admits Phil. "There was a huge number of children at the game, which was great to see, but most importantly the event launched the profile of the Foundation and enabled people to sit up and take note of what we're about.

"It's important that games such as this one leave a legacy, and we have therefore committed some of our funds to legacies in both Munich and Belgrade [in remembrance of the Munich air disaster]. The rest will be invested and each year, over the next fifteen years, we will launch a new programme funded through the proceeds. We hope to have more games, similar to the charity match in the future, but trying to find a free week in the fixtures calendar is not that easy!"

The Foundation is also spreading its wings overseas. United's pre-season tour to Asia in July 2007 gave Sir Alex and his players the opportunity to visit a number of community programmes supported by the Foundation. These included trips to a cancer specialist hospital in Tokyo, orphanages in Seoul and Macau, and a UNICEF-supported project in Guangzhou which gave the players a chance to learn more about how HIV/AIDS is affecting young people, as part of the club's support for the charity's global campaign 'United for Children, Unite against AIDS'.

Since 1999 the United for UNICEF partnership has generated over £2 million and changed the lives of more than one and a half million children in countries including China, India, Thailand, South Africa, Sierra Leone, Mozambique, Afghanistan and Iraq. It has also reached over one

billion people worldwide with important messages about health, education and child protection.

UNICEF Ambassadors including Sir Alex Ferguson, Ryan Giggs, Ole Gunnar Solskjaer, and former players David Beckham and Quinton Fortune are among those who have been on field visits to Thailand, Mozambique, Uganda, India and South Africa to see how the funds raised have been spent to improve children's lives. Other players have demonstrated their support by recording emergency appeal messages, attending events, donating memorabilia for auction and speaking out for the rights of children.

Patrice Evra shows off his skills during a visit to a Korean orphanage in July 2007.

"The club are very active and involved in charity work and being able to make a difference or just even putting a smile on a child's face is very rewarding for all of the players," says Rio Ferdinand.

"I got involved in a special HIV/AIDS campaign with [UNICEF Ambassador] Jemima Khan and it was something I thoroughly enjoyed lending my support to. The UNICEF campaigns are always hard-hitting and as a team we're all committed to helping in any way we can."

"Some of the projects we've seen have been real eye-openers," adds Darren Fletcher. "It's fantastic to see the joy that we can bring to youngsters just by being there. We've also had the opportunity to meet some amazing world figures such as Nelson Mandela, which was an absolute honour. We look upon all the visits as unique experiences and it's great to see our support make a difference."

Making a difference is what the Foundation is continually striving to achieve and United chief executive David Gill is hoping it will have an impact on a global scale over the coming years.

"The Foundation is a key feature of our plans going forward," he insists. "We have opportunities to use our name to help improve people's lives both locally and internationally, and we believe the Foundation will help us to use the funds we generate in the best possible way. I think it has got a very exciting future and hopefully in five to ten years' time the Manchester United Foundation will have a name that is known worldwide."

"The support we've had within the club has been phenomenal," adds Phil Townsend, "from David Gill and Sir Alex to the players and the staff. For me, the Foundation isn't about the amount of publicity and press coverage we receive, it's about the impact we can actually have on the ground. I'd much prefer to see a group of young people inspired by our programmes, than get an article in the media detailing our visit – although both would be great! We can't move away from the human side of what we're doing, that's what must drive us all forward."

VENUE OF DREAMS

12

Old Trafford may be at its most bustling on a matchday, but any thoughts that the stadium's commotion lulls without the presence of Sir Alex Ferguson and his squad are misguided – the ground is actually a hub of activity all year round.

For the past few years the club have worked hard on enhancing the services on offer on non-matchdays in a bid to increase revenue. The man entrusted with coordinating such an operation is director of venue, Karl Evans.

"My prime focus is to make Old Trafford a three-hundred-and-sixty-five-day venue," he insists. "We're continually marketing and enhancing

The club would like to make Old Trafford a 365-day venue.

what we offer on non-matchdays which make up a large percentage of the number of available days per year. Anything we do needs to generate revenue for the club, not necessarily immediately, but there has to be some profit at the end.

"We open our doors to all sorts of different events, exhibitions and seminars which can be worth anything between a hundred and a hundred and fifty thousand pounds. We also host the club's annual Player of the Year Awards ceremony and UNICEF dinner – both of which are attended by Sir Alex and the team – and they have proved to be hugely popular with fans who acquire tables at each event.

"We're also looking at additional things we can do on site using the vast car park space we own," adds Karl, who joined United in July 1988. "For the past few years we've erected a marquee on W3 car park which has played host to United's staff Christmas party, as well as a number of external festive events for other companies – just over twenty thousand people used the facilities during the 2006 Christmas period, which is an impressive number. We also built a temporary ice rink on E2 car park and have tried to introduce some new initiatives in tandem with the museum, the Red Café and the Megastore as well."

Other activities to take place on the pitch – including music concerts and major sporting events – have also helped to generate further funds.

"We got ourselves back into the concert market in July 2007 after staging the Genesis reunion concert," explains Karl. "We've worked hard to get back into that market despite the fierce competition, and we're hoping to stage at least one concert every summer over the coming years.

"We also host the annual Super League Grand Final and we've staged a large number of England internationals and FA Cup semi-finals over the past few years. There have been other high profile events including Soccer Aid [in May 2006] and the Manchester United Foundation match [in March 2007] which were both sell-outs. We have also held some of the auditions for *The X Factor*, which provided us with good coverage on ITV1.

"There are twenty-four function suites in the stadium of different shapes and sizes," he continues. "Add the car park availability to that and, of course, the very fact that we're Manchester United and you've got a very attractive package for a wide range of potential customers.

The UNICEF dinner at Old Trafford in December 2006.

115

There has been huge growth in the club's non-matchday business, and during 2006 we had more than a hundred thousand people through the Old Trafford doors."

Many of those visitors, who visit from both the UK and overseas, will invariably stop off at the club museum, which is situated on level three of North Stand and open seven days a week. They are also likely to attend one of the daily stadium tours which, at peak times, can take place up to 46 times a day.

"We get between 210,000 and 230,000 visitors a year – including some of the current team and ex-players – round the museum, although when United won the Treble our figures shot up to 275,000," reveals Museum curator Mark Wylie, who joined the club in August 1991.

"When I first started the museum was situated between the South Stand tunnel and the East Stand. But during the nineties the number of visitors went through the roof and it soon became obvious that we had to relocate. That we did and the current museum, which cost four million pounds to build, opened in April 1998.

"We have a rolling programme which involves re-cleaning, re-displaying and re-captioning items," continues Mark, who was part of the museum team that picked up the award for the Large Visitor Attraction in 2005 at the Marketing Manchester Tourism Awards. "Throughout the year we'll subtly change things in the display cases. About eighty per cent of the items we own are not on display because we simply haven't got enough space. We've got just over twenty thousand objects in our collection, the majority of which are paper based – programmes, tickets, magazines and other ephemera. But there's probably only about two thousand on show.

"Some items are always on display, while others are put out for a limited period. We also have a programme of temporary exhibitions, usually around two major ones each year, with up to five smaller presentations as well. The smaller ones react to what is happening around the club at certain times such as when Sir Alex celebrated his twentieth anniversary at United, and the death of George Best."

Players and managers, past and present, happily loan their personal honours to the museum for display.

"The largest number of items that we have on loan is probably

from one of Gary Neville, Peter Schmeichel, Denis Irwin, Ryan Giggs and Sir Alex," explains Mark. "They have all been very willing to assist the museum and let us display their treasured memorabilia.

"Some of our most popular items include Wayne Rooney's ripped debut shirt and the one Eric Cantona was wearing on that infamous night at Selhurst Park [in January 1995]. We've also got Ole Gunnar Solskjaer's boots from the 1999 European Cup final and Sir Bobby Charlton's World Cup medal. The most poignant item we have is the telegram that Duncan Edwards sent from Munich to his landlady saying that the team wouldn't be flying home. Of course, that didn't turn out to be the case and it's something that will always stick in my mind."

The museum at Old Trafford attracts well over 200,000 visitors each year.

13

JUST THE TICKET

The scramble for tickets to watch United in action and the subsequent bedlam it creates in the Old Trafford Ticket Office is a weekly occurrence. The demand to see the Reds far outweighs supply on virtually every occasion (on average the club turn away around 6,000 fans per home game) and ultimately leaves many supporters with little choice but to cheer on the team from their own front room rather than in the flesh.

Steven Hall, ticketing and membership general manager, is in charge of ensuring every United fan has a fair chance of seeing their heroes in action, but, as he explains, trying to keep everyone happy has its challenges.

Fans queue patiently for their chance to watch the Reds in action.

"That's what we try to do, but it's not always possible because people get very emotionally involved in applying for tickets," says Steven, who oversees a team of around 35 full-time staff split across five departments within the ticketing and membership set-up. "Managing people's expectations is another big part of the job. The demand is so huge for tickets and it far exceeds supply, so it's up to us to try and water down those expectations so people aren't left disappointed."

Since the expansion of Old Trafford to a 76,000 capacity, there has been a substantial increase in the number of executive members (as of May 2007 the total figure was 8,000), and season ticket-holders (57,000), while the club's membership scheme – One United – also has a considerable subscription list of 130,000.

"Those members are all entitled to apply for one ticket each for every home game," explains Steven. "We accept applications from them six weeks in advance by phone or online. We no longer accept postal applications as everything is done by automation nowadays. They are all put into one pot and a random ballot takes place.

"Typically only half of our members will apply for at least one game during the season. People become members for all kinds of reasons, not just so they're able to apply for tickets; some fans just want an association with the club. Others will apply for every game but we try and make it a fair split so everyone gets a chance to see the team.

"The automation system we now use for ticket applications allows us to notice any trends. For instance if a member has applied for five games but hasn't yet got a ticket, we'll try and accommodate their next request. Some people get quite irate if they miss out on certain tickets, but sometimes it might simply be down to the fact that their credit card has expired. We aim to work out the fairest process where as many people as possible are successful."

United have over 150 Supporters' Clubs based within the UK and around the world (they need to have at least 50 One United Members in order to become a branch), and the club reserve a pool of 1,200 tickets for them for each home game. From the start of the 2006/07 season the club introduced a season ticket waiting list for members. As of May 2007 there were around 15,000 on the register but, as with the figures for executive members and season ticket holders, it is a number that is likely to fluctuate at the start of each campaign.

"With price increases and changing circumstances there is always an inevitable churn before the start of every season," says Steven. "Those tickets which are not renewed will be offered to the first people on the waiting list and so on, so the numbers will vary.

"From the start of the 2007/08 season every season ticket holder became part of the automatic Cup Scheme which means they have to commit to buying a ticket for every cup match at Old Trafford. The cup games are included in the season ticket package for executive members anyway. This change will mean cup tickets are less likely to end up on general sale, as some Champions League matches have done in the past, because fifty-seven thousand tickets will be guaranteed to be sold, on top of the eight thousand executive seats."

Aside from dealing with the ticketing logistics for home games, the Ticket Office also deal with applications for domestic and European away games, as well as cup finals and on occasion pre-season tours and friendlies.

The application process for away matches and cup finals in particular is a hugely contentious issue. The fact that there simply aren't enough tickets to go round means the procedure by which successful applicants are determined is one that is highly scrutinised by every fan and his dog.

"Our allocation for domestic away games is usually around three thousand tickets," explains Steven, who joined the club in August 1993. "Everyone on the automatic Cup Scheme can apply for away games and on average we receive around four thousand applications for every one. Between two and three hundred are set aside for players and directors, while seven hundred are put away for executive members who receive a maximum of two tickets each. Three-quarters of the remaining allocation, around two thousand, will go to the loyalty pot, and then the standard pot.

"The loyalty pot is made up of those fans who have applied for every away game from the Middlesbrough away game [in December 2002] onwards. They have an eighty-five per cent success rate of getting a ticket for every away match. In the past if some fans dropped out of the loyalty pot we would always top it back up to a figure of around fourteen hundred. But the Fans' Forum decided to change that in 2007 so

more tickets are now available for the standard pot, which includes fans who apply on an ad-hoc basis for away games. There was in the region of eleven hundred in the loyalty pot at the start of the 2007/08 season.

"Successful applicants in both pots are decided by a ballot, which can take around four or five hours to run. We have the ability to implement certain rules within the system to weight the ballot in favour of certain people, such as those who have all the credits needed to apply for specific tickets. People may also have price preferences too so we need to consider that as well.

Some of the lucky ones celebrate another United goal.

Issues related to persistent standing by fans during away matches have seen United's allocation for away games being cut by some clubs, notably Middlesbrough and Charlton.

"It's happening more and more throughout the game," says Steven. "But inevitably our club seems to be targeted more than others because of our high profile and also because not every club has the same following as we do – we always sell all of our allocation for away games."

The same can usually be said for the majority of the team's European away matches which are open to executive members, season ticket-holders and members to apply for.

"We don't get as many applications for European away games as domestic ones but they are still very popular," explains Steven. "For the bigger matches we usually receive around four to five thousand tickets. We always ensure the fans that actually apply for tickets do actually go themselves, by handing out the tickets at the destination. People who travel to every European away game get priority for the matches during the latter stages."

Ready for action.

Part Four

MATCHDAY AT THE THEATRE

"I feel at home at Old Trafford. I feel we've taken it back as a fortress, as it used to be. Opposition players look forward to it but they fear it in a way. In the back of their minds they're thinking, 'imagine if they're on song today, we'll be in for a hard day.'"

OLE GUNNAR SOLSKJAER

SETTING THE STAGE

14

For a seasoned visitor to Old Trafford, the matchday experience might last a touch over two hours. The rush to get through the turnstiles before kick-off, queuing for a half-time pie and then a final whistle dash back to the car can substantially trim a day at the Theatre of Dreams.

For Old Trafford's staff, however, the day often begins before the sun has clocked in. Supporter protection is absolutely paramount for United, so the first stadium safety checks begin at 7 a.m. on a home matchday – regardless of the kick-off time.

"Over the course of a season we deal with in excess of two and a

A fan waits outside the stadium as Old Trafford is prepared.

quarter million people on matchdays at Old Trafford. Managing seventy-six thousand fans is the equivalent of looking after a small town," says stadium safety officer Arthur Roberts. "Thankfully I work with an exceptional team of stewards, supervisors and other United staff who make up the safety team.

"Without the good behaviour of ninety-nine per cent of the fans we could not manage the stadium. Unfortunately, there is a small minority who misbehave and give football a bad name. It's our job to identify those offenders and make sure our stewards and security personnel are properly trained to deal with them. My job is to coordinate what is a huge team of extremely experienced stewards, supervisors, safety personnel and maintenance personnel. We must ensure we look after the first fan that walks through the turnstiles, through to the last supporter that leaves the ground."

The culture of fan safety has been altered irrevocably in recent times, due in part to the evolution of blame and claim culture, and the fallout from the 1989 Hillsborough disaster.

"Before I joined United, I was the Police Commander of Old Trafford and Stretford for eight years and worked very closely with the club during that time," explains Roberts. "Lord Justice Taylor's report on the Hillsborough disaster saw the whole emphasis regarding the safety management of football stadiums change. His report deemed that it was the sole responsibility of clubs to safeguard the wellbeing of any fan that entered their stadium, and United asked me to look at the impact that would have upon the management of Old Trafford.

"I was in from the very beginning and was therefore able to have an input into the design, the construction, and the management of the stadium. Those three integral parts formed the building blocks of how we went about redeveloping the ground while also retaining the essential character of Old Trafford.

"Things are constantly happening before, during and after the match. It can be all sorts of things from a lost child, to a blocked toilet, to a medical emergency or public disorder."

A 2,000-strong throng of matchday staff ensure that every aspect of the stadium is absolutely ready for the arrival of 76,000 spectators. Programme sellers flogging copies of United Review, maintenance men

fixing broken taps and kiosk staff pouring hot Bovril, are all united in their endeavours. Just as the more recognisable first team do their utmost to work together for success on the field, so the backroom staff toil away in sync to ensure the matchday experience passes off without a hitch.

United's all-seeing eye in the stadium control room.

Club secretary Ken Ramsden, a United employee since 1960, takes great pride in the dutiful nature of the club's matchday staff, not least because they share an ethos he has lived by throughout his entire working career.

"There are really good staff at Manchester United and everybody does a job," he says. "When I came and the late Les Olive was secretary, he had all the keys and he would go around all the toilets on matchdays and make sure they were clean. He would make sure there was toilet paper and soap in them all. The secretary of Manchester United was doing that before every home game!

"Now the world has moved on. We've got departments for things like that, and I stand back sometimes and see how it all comes together. It's as if it's by magic, but it's not, it's by experience and expertise. People know their jobs. You might have fifty people doing a small or not so small job, but they all do them and it all comes together. It comes with training, practice, expertise and having big games regularly.

"We've got a relatively big staff compared to some clubs and everyone's got huge pride. If there was a broken seat, they want it fixing. If there's a dirty seat, they want it cleaning. During the first half all the concourses are cleaned, as is the area outside the ground, so that when you go for a cup of tea at half time everything is pretty much spotless.

"When I go to some European venues on a pre-match visit ahead of the team's game out there, they might have had a game a fortnight before and the place is absolutely filthy. There are newspapers everywhere, dirty seats and I just think 'this couldn't happen in Manchester'. It could be a cultural thing, but there's huge pride here. This is a club-owned stadium, people here feel as if they own the club. And in a sense they do because they're the people of Manchester United.

"The fans, the staff and the players – everyone wants to impress and the chest bursts out with pride," he continues. "We've had rugby league matches here which have been beamed all around the world. To sit there at tea-time and say that somebody in Australia or New Zealand is watching Old Trafford gives a fantastic sense of purpose and achievement. I think that's what everybody feels here."

Pride and ambition are the building blocks of much of the United mantra – there are no half measures. The redevelopment of Old Trafford's quadrants, completed in August 2006, was a sizeable step in the club's ongoing aim to refine and hone one of world football's finest venues, increasing the capacity and also revolutionising United's matchday hospitality facilities.

"We have around nine thousand executive visitors every matchday, which in truth, is more than most clubs could ever dream about," says director of venue Karl Evans. "Eight thousand of those are regulars, while we sell another thousand seats on a match-by-match hospitality basis. Multiply that by, say, twenty-five matches and you get a figure of around quarter of a million who enjoy the corporate experience on a matchday each season.

"The quadrants have provided us with the opportunity to not only enhance what we already offer, but also introduce some new styles and imagination to the new suites. We opened ten restaurants through the expansion. Not only do they have matchday appeal, they also have non-matchday appeal because of their fantastic views of the pitch and across Salford Quays.

"We offer a range of different options for pre-match dining," adds Karl. "We have a fine dining restaurant which has been hugely popular with customers. Fine dining at a football stadium is not a typical combination, but we did a lot of research into it and the response has been very positive. We also link up with Lancashire County Cricket Ground on the hospitality side and overall the whole operation has been hugely successful.

"As the director of venue, everyone who visits the stadium interacts with members of my team, both on matchdays and non-matchdays. So I feel a huge sense of pride when a big event goes well. The role certainly has its challenges, but it's something I very much enjoy. I'm here every matchday, and I see it right through from the catering briefing, which takes places five hours before kick-off, until the last person leaves at the end of the day."

"Everyone who visits Old Trafford can see what a magnificent

The food and the atmosphere in United's corporate hospitality suites are something truly special.

stadium it is and there's a real atmosphere about the place," says chief executive David Gill. "Quite rightly it is recognised as one of the most iconic venues in the world of sport.

"The new Wembley is fantastic but there is something unique about Manchester United and Old Trafford that you can't replicate. It's a wonderful stadium in my eyes. You can become blasé when you're here everyday, but you only need to look at people's faces when they come for the first time, to see how it can take your breath away."

The ground's hulking architecture enshrouds row upon row of seating, all centred towards the Old Trafford turf. The stage is the centrepiece of any theatre, so the preparation which goes into readying the pitch is an absolutely integral aspect of a home matchday – not to mention an endless task for head groundsman Tony Sinclair and his eight-man team.

"We'll actually cut the pitch three times on the day of the game, twice lengthways and once across at a length of twenty-six millimetres," reveals Sinclair. "We then get the marking out done because we have to give the paint an hour to dry and then start building up the moisture, which we'll be doing right up until kick-off.

"Different parts of the pitch have different amounts of water. We wouldn't water the south side as much as the north, because the north sits in the sun all day long. So the south side has less water so that you don't create any algae or an anaerobic build-up. We know the moisture on the south side will hold fine without as much water as the north side.

"We've got forty sprinkler heads which come on two at a time. We don't just put them all on for five minutes each. One section might be two minutes, one might be two and a half, one might be three and a half. We'll get soil and test each area just to see how moist the area is underneath before deciding what we'll do. It's strange, some people still don't understand what's involved in the whole thing.

"Some people say 'you don't roll when it's damp', but not everything we do is in accordance with nature. But at the end of the day, the pitch is the stage. That's what the team play on and it's what they want that matters. We might go a week without water, just to let the roots go and find the moisture. Then we could get to the Saturday and spend six hours watering it. Then the grass plant thinks it's had five or six days of

Head groundsman Tony Sinclair tends to the Old Trafford turf.

water, so we'll lay off it for a few days. It's a plant. We don't always follow nature, but that's the nature of what we're doing.

"Our aim is to present the pitch in the best possible state for the team and the manager, even if we're going against nature. We can't turn up in the morning and just say 'oh it's a bit drizzly, so we're not going to cut today because nature says'. Somehow I don't think the boss would appreciate it if we went to him on the night of a game with that excuse. If you were going to cut your lawn tomorrow and it was raining, you wouldn't do it. That doesn't mean we won't cut the pitch. What they want, goes."

Often to the supporters' bemusement, Tony and his team continue to water the pitch right up until kick-off. Their fears, he reveals, are far from well-founded.

"Sometimes supporters see us watering just before kick-off and at half time and you can hear them saying 'I can't believe they're watering the pitch now', but people have to understand the pitch is ninety-five per cent sand," he says. "I still hear people saying that it'll make the pitch muddy, and they couldn't be any further from the truth. It's so sand-based that the water enhances it.

"When we water at half time, yes it puts some zip on the leaf and helps the team, but it also enhances the pitch because it weights the sand down. That also helps to decrease the risk of injury because it prevents the pitch from becoming harder. If we didn't water it then it would dry out beyond belief and get firmer and bouncier, so we are doing it for the right reasons."

STARS OF THE SHOW

15

The players who ply their trade on the groundstaff's handiwork are undoubtedly the stars of the show. Given the celebrity culture of modern football, player and staff security has never been more important. As such, United's relationship with Controlled Event Solutions (CES) is a vital component of a smooth-running matchday.

Over 400 CES staff provide safekeeping and ensure each matchday remains in order, as well as providing non-matchday security at Old Trafford events and around the stadium on a daily basis.

It's CES who accompany and look after the players at each match:

home, away and abroad. Old Trafford games naturally require more of the company's staff – with manned guarding, CCTV and detection dogs.

Trained by ex-UK Special Forces staff, close protection officers provide the traditional bodyguard protection for United's superstar players, including on their transfer from hotel to stadium.

The team will usually stay in a hotel the night before a home game, often when the players have been away on international duty, in order to make them feel that they are part of the same team again. Upon arriving at Old Trafford via coach and CES escort, the players filter into the dressing room, before taking in a pre-match meal of the individual's choice, usually three hours before kick-off.

"Generally it's down to the comfort of your digestive system," says dietician Trevor Lea. "With training every day and regular matches, the players get to know the kind of things they like to eat. One player might like beans on toast, another could like cereal, and another might want soup or chicken breast, pasta and a little tomato sauce.

"There are many different things, but the primary concern is that each player eats something that they know isn't going to upset their stomach. That generally means nothing spicy, just something easy to digest. It could be fruit salad and a yoghurt, toast and jam, or rice and chicken. It's very individual, there's nothing set. If there was, then it would be a secret!

"They do need to go into games with their muscles full of carbohydrates, but you don't get that from the pre-match meal. It takes about twenty-four hours to really get into your muscles, so they're eating like that all the time because they have training every day. The pre-match meal is just for comfort."

Having eaten, the squad will then mill around backstage. They can be found reading the papers in the Players' Lounge, distributing their match tickets or playing music in the dressing room, the latter of which is a bone of contention as contrasting tastes collide.

"We play music in the dressing room which creates a nice atmosphere," says Ole Gunnar Solskjaer. "Everyone more or less has their own routines and they all know how to focus and get one hundred per cent ready for kick-off. The wrong people pick the music though!

"Sometimes it's all right, but sometimes it's better to put your iPod

Cristiano Ronaldo, Ji-sung Park and John O'Shea relax in the lounge ahead of a match.

on! We're all different though. Sometimes Gary [Neville] chooses the music before and after the game, sometimes Rio does, or Cristiano puts his own thing on, so it's different players. I think my music is a little bit too special for the likes of them to enjoy. I'm into a little more rock and roll than the pop music some of the lads are into. I need some energy before a game!"

The Norwegian's assertion that he enjoys an acquired taste in music is backed up by Rio Ferdinand, the man seen by many players as the team's unofficial matchday DJ.

"Ole played the worst CD I've ever heard one time," laughs the towering centre back. "It was a mixture of crazy rock and completely off-key music. I couldn't even explain to you what it was, but it never got played again! I don't think anyone has got particularly bad taste in music, that was just a bad choice from Ole.

"Before a game I'll listen to anything that gets me a bit rocking, like old jungle, old house, and garage or some really hard rap on my iPod. That helps to get me psyched up for the match. Before a game either myself, Wazza or Gary will put something on the main iPod in the dressing room."

"It all depends," smiles John O'Shea. "Sometimes Rio goes a bit too deep into his R&B and rap stuff, it doesn't mix well with some of us. Patrice [Evra] too, we've had some great dance music from Jimmy's nightclub in Monaco which he introduced us to! We've got a good mix."

Music is merely part of the pre-match hubbub, vying for attention alongside jovial banter, stray footballs and – of course – TV.

"Our dressing room has always been a noisy and lively place before a game," says Gary Neville. "Some of the lads might be doing keepie-uppies or watching the television – which is always on up until we go out for the warm-up – while others might put some music on. Once we come back in from the warm-up the dressing room quietens down a bit as everyone starts to fully focus on the match."

As club captain and one of the team's elder statesmen, Neville is in a position of authority – although he has put his own stamp on the captain's role since replacing previous incumbent Roy Keane in 2005.

"I'm nothing like any of the captains I've played under," says Neville. "It would be impossible to emulate past captains of this club, you've just got to do what you do and be yourself. I haven't changed the way I train or the way I speak to players on the pitch since I became skipper. I've always thought about what's best for the team even when I wasn't captain and I've just continued to do that.

"I'll very rarely say something to the whole team in the dressing room before a game. But on occasion I might pass on one or two instructions to individual defenders. I always feel that during that last hour leading up to kick-off, most of your preparation for the game is done."

As kick-off approaches, the team are shown a short video to familiarise them with their rivals. Although the end product is usually no more than 10 or 15 minutes long, the amount of research that is lavished upon their opponents is almost unfathomable.

"We have people who analyse games, teams, individuals, all the time, that's an ongoing thing," says coach Mike Phelan. "We have a structure in place whereby all the direct first team coaches see our opponents regularly. Obviously we have regular contact with scouts and people who have seen what's developing, and we produce DVDs if we feel as though the players need to see it.

"The coaches and manager will always see it, so we have good information coming to us all the time. It's how we use it that's the important thing. Because football is on the telly twenty-four hours a day, you can watch a game in South America the morning after the night before, so you can always keep in touch with games. If we wanted to be really boring we could watch it all the time, but you have to have a life as well. We're specific in what we need to see and then occasionally something else might come up that we need to cover. It's fed down the line through the system and hopefully we don't miss anything.

"It's the most important area now in the game," insists Mike. "For a start it's cost-effective. If you can stay here and watch all the games on TV, it's not as time consuming for the coaches because we don't have to travel anywhere. That allows us more time with the players to prepare them. We could be all over the place, but we have people who are always working in that area, who produce information for us to take the final look at, and then we relay that to the team or the individual player. Nowadays, that side of things is very important because there's a lot of money in the game now. The bigger clubs, the ones in the major, major leagues, all have this kind of facility.

"Depending on the size of the game, it requires different levels of treatment. Because we get games coming thick and fast, we may only look slightly into a match and instead rely on our team to do the business. We know the strengths of our team so we don't really need to go into that much depth, we just concentrate on ourselves. When we get into the bigger domestic games or the European games, more detail is required. When it's Europe you're up against sides you don't see as regularly as those in the Premiership.

"We do focus and put a lot more energy into those fixtures. They're bigger games, bigger stakes. I'm not belittling what we do in the league because that's unbelievably important. We do have a regular load of information in the league, but it's different in Europe. You get bits of information, but you're not able to monitor them as often as you need to because you usually don't have the time. So we just pick up and make it as intense as we can for two or three days, and then we relax and move on to the next one. We always have data which we can refer to, so we get to know everything that's going on."

Once the players have been briefed on their opponents, Sir Alex Ferguson names his starting side and substitutes, who stretch and see head physiotherapist Rob Swire for any required strappings, before getting changed for the warm-up. Tony Coton and the goalkeepers take to the field first, around 50 minutes before kick-off, with the goalkeeping coach's mantra very much one of letting the player dictate the routine.

"The older, established keepers like Barthez, Schmeichel or Van der Sar, who have been here, I just tell them: I'm here for you, I'm not going to try and change you, if you've got anything you prefer to do, talk to me and I'll tell you if I think it's all right," he explains.

"Edwin went through his pre-match warm-up with me [when he first joined], and he prefers the majority of the warm-up just for him. I therefore come out earlier with the substitute goalkeeper, get him done and then send him off with either Garry [Armer] or one of the physios to do some passing and working on his touch. He needs to do that to keep him warm, then he comes back in and serves for Edwin with me."

Coton and the substitute stopper will then warm up the starting keeper with some shooting. On the occasions that the former United

and City keeper scores, his reaction is generally akin to that of a man who has just accidentally shredded a winning lottery ticket.

"I'm not looking to score," he confides. "I'm looking to build their confidence up. So if I do mishit one and it flies in the top corner then I'm not happy with it, because that's not what I'm intending to do. I'm looking to get it within range for them, probably full extension, but not to score."

While Coton is preparing the goalkeepers, the outfield players take to the field soon after to begin their own warm-up, led by skipper Gary Neville.

"For the past few seasons I've taken the first five minutes of the warm-up," says Neville. "I do the same thing every week and it helps to get everyone going, although the lads tell me I put them through quite a hard session! The warm-up is one part of the game that's changed

Stand-in skipper Rio Ferdinand gets ready in the tunnel to lead the team out on to the Old Trafford pitch.

greatly. I used to go out there and do my own thing before every match, but now we all do it together, which is much better.

"We stretch together and play a little five-a-side, before going off and doing a bit by ourselves at the end. Some of the lads will work on their passing, while others will focus on heading or shooting. I always warm up with the same players at Old Trafford, and wherever I'm playing – be it home or away – I'll always warm up in the right back position. I like to stand in my position and accept the ball there so I can get a feel for it. It's something I've always done."

Although Neville leads the opening chapter of the pre-game exercise, Tony Strudwick is still the man in charge of ensuring the players are absolutely ready for action.

"I may change parts of the warm-up if it's particularly cold or hot, but the overall structure remains the same throughout the majority of the season for every game, home and away," he says. "After Gary has taken the opening part of the warm-up, the players do a stretching session on the spot for around ten minutes. The ten outfield players who are starting the match will then take part in some specific exercises with me for around five minutes. These include skipping and sprinting which helps to ensure their body temperature is at the correct level.

"Once that is complete, the ten will split into two groups of five and spend three or four minutes playing a mini-game. For the final five minutes of the warm-up, the players are free to work on anything they want. The strikers often work on their shooting, while the defenders spend time on their passing or their heading.

"Normally, I don't like to repeat too many things during the week leading up to a game in training because I think it's important for the players to keep doing different things. But before a match, during the warm-up, I like to keep a regular structure. I think it helps the players focus their mind on the match. Everything about matchday needs to be routine."

When the players have returned to the dressing room after the warm-up, around ten minutes before kick-off, the mood takes on a steely, focused tone. Outside, the strains of John Squire's guitar pierce the Manchester air, Ian Brown's vocals echo over a background of climaxing drums and building bass. It's show time.

16 SHOWTIME

For United's players, the sounds of the Stone Roses anthem "This is the One" are a source of inspiration, the perfect fanfare to signal the start of battle.

"'This is the One' is cherished by the players," says Ole Gunnar Solskjaer. "I think it was Gary [Neville] who started with the Stone Roses, and I think everyone realises it's the heart of Manchester. We're in Manchester, the Stone Roses were a Manchester band, and I think we all feel something for that song, and that band for that matter. I've grown to like them.

"I'd say I'm a bit of a Manc," he laughs, before adding an unexpectedly

With room for more than 100 journalists, the United press box is always packed.

S126

colloquial "oh aye". "I've been here so long, my kids have grown up here. When my little boy plays on his PSP [PlayStation Portable] he sometimes has the Stone Roses on too, so I encourage that. He's a Manc as well!"

Two former Roses, lead singer Brown and bassist Mani, are still regular attendees at Old Trafford. They, like the rest of the gathered masses, know their song is the cue for the Reds to take to the field. Now's the time for nerves, but if there are any, you can't see it in the players. Judging by captain Gary Neville's face, he could be at home reading the paper, such is the dearth of discernible emotion.

"I'm just thinking of the game when I'm stood in the tunnel waiting to lead the team out," he reveals. "I try to think about the simple things that I want to do well in the match, such as making sure my passing is good and my defending is solid so I don't give the opposition any encouragement. I'll also be thinking about my opponent and what I need to do to deal with him. To be honest most of the thinking will have been done by that point, but during those last few minutes in the tunnel I'll be focusing on two or three simple aspects to make sure I start the game well.

"Walking out of the tunnel on to the Old Trafford pitch is still the best thing that's ever happened to me in my life. It's a great feeling and I'll probably only truly realise it when it's gone. To play at such a great stadium in front of so many people week in, week out is just brilliant."

Of course, not everybody can make it to see the Reds in action every week. With a worldwide fanbase of millions, 76,000 seats don't stretch that far. The vast majority will tune in to watch games on TV – typically Sky Sports in the UK – and the broadcasting process is one which begins well in advance of each match.

Up to ten outside broadcast (OB) trucks arrive at Old Trafford the day before the game, unravelling up to five miles of cable which is put into place around the stadium. Next to arrive on site are the broadcast computing equipment and graphics, which completes the setting-up process.

The technical crew arrive early on the matchday morning, along with production staff who are part of a 130-strong workforce for the game. Each live game is assigned its own match director who has his or her

The Sky Sports team get ready to go on air.

own truck from which to view every image projected from the 22 cameras around the stadium, and decide what the watching public will see on their screens.

Over at Sky Sports HQ, there are a number of dedicated staff working on the channel's interactive coverage, while the matchday studio houses presenters and pundits to mull over events and chew the metaphorical post-match fat.

There are alternative media facets at work on a home matchday too. Old Trafford's press box holds over 100 journalists – mainly newspaper writers and radio commentators – including the club's official media. Club website ManUtd.com provides live text commentary and full match report and reaction, Manchester United Radio gives live audio commentary and post-match post-mortem, while MUTV gives all the pre-match build-up and in-depth aftermath with a host of ex-players.

The media's collective role is to be the eyes and ears of those who cannot attend the match. For those who are there, shoehorned into 76,000 seats, the role is to provide the perfect soundtrack for the players to make memories, and in no way do the squad or Sir Alex Ferguson underestimate the collective role those in the stands can play.

"Some nights the atmosphere really is unbelievable, whether it be at home to Liverpool or Chelsea or the really big games in Europe," says John O'Shea. "It's just a special place, particularly on European nights. It's up to us to give them something to get going about. That's the pressure we enjoy and hopefully we do that on most occasions! It makes you want to be out on that pitch doing everything you can for the team. That's where every player wants to be."

"The fans can make a hell of a difference," adds Sir Alex. "There's no doubt about that. I think human nature means you respond to emotions, and the emotions of fans in games like Blackburn and Roma last season [2006/07] were absolutely magnificent, and the players responded accordingly."

Playing in front of so many supporters on such a regular basis can be a culture shock for new faces in the squad, and Nemanja Vidic is still stunned by United's popularity since joining the club in January 2006.

"Every week I'm amazed that we play in front of 76,000 fans at Old Trafford – it's unbelievable," says the Serbian defender. "I'd never ever experienced it before. Even for the matches with the so-called smaller sides, the stadium is full. I remember talking to a few of the lads in the dressing room before a Carling Cup match soon after I'd joined and asking them how many fans they thought would be at the match.

"I thought there would be around 15,000 or so, but they turned round to me and said it'll be nearer 60,000 and they were right, I couldn't believe it! You have everything you need at this club – a great stadium, great fans and great people."

One man who has enjoyed a relationship of mutual appreciation with the Red Army is Wayne Rooney. He is the perfect example of how the rapport between crowd and players works. They sing to inspire him, he inspires them to sing.

"It's brilliant," smiles the striker. "To have that many people singing your name and shouting for you is an unbelievable feeling. I'm proud of that and hopefully I can keep exciting the fans so they keep urging me on.

"When you hear them sing your name during a game it lifts you, excites you and makes you want to do well for them as well. Old Trafford is a great place to play, the atmosphere is good and it's one of the best stadiums in the world. I'm sure if you built another Old Trafford on top, they'd probably be able to fill that as well. To be able to play there week in, week out is brilliant for me, and a great honour."

"I feel at home at Old Trafford," adds Ole Gunnar Solskjaer. "I feel we've taken it back as a fortress, as it used to be. It sounds like a cliché, but at Old Trafford now opposition players look forward to it but they fear it in a way. I think in the back of their minds they're thinking, 'just imagine if they're on song today, we'll be in for a hard afternoon.'"

While the fans' cares barely extend beyond the final score and the bigger picture of United's season, those on the home bench are watching events unfold in a different way.

Kit manager Albert Morgan is ready for any potential material hitches, armed with spare shirts, shorts, socks and boots aplenty.

"I take about a hundred shirts to every game, two sets of shorts, two sets of everything really," he says. "I have two sets of short sleeve shirts and two sets of long sleeve shirts for every player. Depending on the weather, some players will swap about with short and long sleeves, so you've got to be prepared for every eventuality. We take three pairs of boots for each player too. The motto in the laundry room is 'cover your arse!' Three or four of them will wear a vest or cycling shorts, but they're all pretty straight-forward. You get to know what each individual player likes to wear.

"As a United fan it's fantastic to watch every game from the bench. But I watch it from a different perspective to anyone else. If a player starts looking at their boots I immediately think 'what's happened here?' and I'm wondering if that player wants a new pair.

"Many a time I can be looking at something fifteen yards behind the play and suddenly a roar goes up and we've scored and I missed the goal! That happens quite often. During one game Vida [Nemanja Vidic]

Albert Morgan hard at work in the dressing room getting everything ready for the big game.

had his boots ripped after he had been tackled and I had to dash over with his spare pair. So I've got to be alert all the time and be ready to act on anything. You can never settle until that final whistle goes."

Fitness coach Tony Strudwick is also on tenterhooks as he ensures the readiness of the United substitutes. "During a match it's my job to ensure they're prepared in case they're needed," he says. "I therefore tell them when to go and warm up during periods in the match. For games at Old Trafford, I organise for five exercise bikes to be brought into the dressing room at half time so the substitutes can do a fifteen-minute warm-up to get their body temperatures to the correct level."

Fellow bench-warmers club doctor Steve McNally and physio Rob Swire are perpetually poised, ready to take to the field to tend any injured players.

When pressed as to the contents of his medical bag, Swire laughs: "There's not that much really, and as the years go by it's getting less and

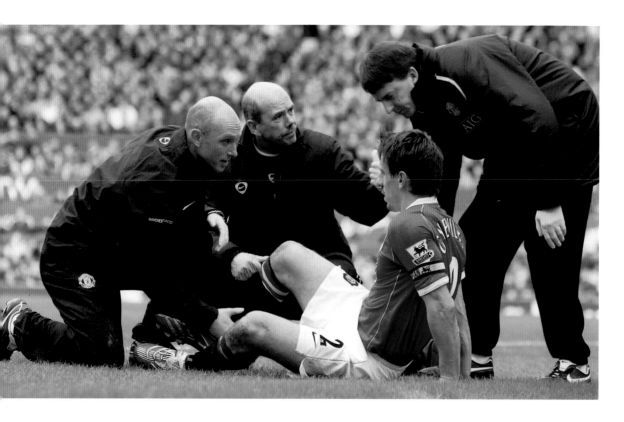

Skipper Gary Neville
receives attention from
United's medical team.

less. When you first start out, you put everything in for every eventuality, but there are things you never use.

"We're lucky that we've got paramedics at home and away games, so they'll have the equipment for serious injuries, splints, neck collars and the likes. I have two water bottles, a sponge – although I don't like to use it that much, and it's not magic. The sponge was used a lot years ago so the players at the time expected it, so you felt you had to have one in case they were calling for it. But now I've not been asked for a sponge for years. They're not hygienic, you can't just go slapping a dirty sponge on, it's not going to be clean. I do have water bottles so I can squirt water on the injuries to clean the muck out. But the majority of the water is just drunk by the players during a break.

"I have various strappings and tapes too. If someone has a dislocated finger you might want to strap it up, again the same with an ankle. Bandages for holding dressings on for head wounds. Vaseline to stop blood flowing, it clogs it all up for a while. As a temporary measure it does stop the blood oozing and then you can hand the player over to the doctor to sort out! It keeps it clean, tidy and a little bit sealed."

Swire's role is often to perform a patch-up job which allows the players to rejoin the fray. Placebos, while doing nothing for the actual injury, can be just the quick fix required to facilitate the player's return to action.

"The players might sometimes ask for a cold spray," he says. "I don't particularly like using them because it just gets the skin cold, perhaps taking the pain away, but it doesn't do anything for the injury. In the heat of the moment the players sometimes want something and they might not be happy if you don't have it, so you put it in. So I have a cold spray and a hot spray. The player might have a stiff back, and a bit of heat on it might help. It's more about keeping them happy and playing the game as much as treating anything. It's treating the mind more than the injury."

Club doctor Steve McNally is similarly focused on any potential medical situations.

"Once the match starts I'm obviously available for any medical emergencies or injuries that require my input," he says. "Rob and I have a signalling mechanism. We don't tend to keep in radio contact because it doesn't always work that well and you can end up with a lot of interference. The important thing is to assess the situation in a calm and collected manner and then make your decision as to whether a player can carry on or not. There are times when I won't wait for Rob's signal if it seems apparent that I'll be needed, perhaps for a head injury or if someone is unconscious or if a player looks to have an obvious deformity such as a dislocation.

"Quite often when you run on the pitch to assess a player you don't always get much sense out of them, particularly if they're a little dazed or stunned from a tackle or a clash of some sort which may have left them in a lot of pain. It's sometimes just a question of observation from my point of view, until the players are able to tell me a bit more about how they're feeling.

"When I'm sat on the bench I'm not following the ball. Instead I'll be looking at players who might have picked up a knock or who have just come back from injury. When things go well for the team you can get caught up in the emotion of it all and our bench is usually quite lively! You do feel part of the team and it would therefore be very hard to just sit there impassively and not enjoy any successes or also share in disappointments."

Sir Alex and his coaching staff, meanwhile, are busy ensuring that all their best-laid pre-match plans are coming to fruition.

"We watch for certain things," says Mike Phelan. "Things may be delivered in the manager's team talk and we will look to see if we're producing those in the game. But then the match can throw up different things. It may not be going the way you want it to, so we have to come up with certain ideas among ourselves, discuss changing this or that or nothing, and make decisions as it's happening.

"Things do change, for instance if we get a formation wrong or they don't play the players we expected. Then we revise the information and plan accordingly, in which case we might give the players different last-minute instructions. That depends on the quality of the players. The ones we have here are very good at changing tactics. As long as we get that information to them, they carry it out."

"During games, once the ball comes past the halfway line I'm looking at the defenders in relation to where the keeper is," says Tony Coton. "What's the distance, are they too close to him, is he not keeping them far enough out, does he have enough space to work in if the ball comes through, is he talking enough, can he be a little bit quicker with his distribution?"

For those players who don't make the squad, whether through injury, suspension, or non-selection, the order of the day is a seat in the Directors' Box. Somewhat predictably, it's not a vantage point many of them want to sample too often.

"Watching from the stands when you're injured or suspended can be very frustrating," admits Gary Neville. "I sometimes end up commentating on the game rather than watching it because I'm so desperate for the lads to do well! You end up shouting and screaming from your seat and I think you're more anxious and nervous when you're not playing. Once I know we're going to win, however, I feel okay."

Assistant manager Carlos Queiroz spends all game ensuring that the blueprint for success he and his colleagues have plotted during training are unfolding accordingly.

The best seat in the house? The coaching staff and substitutes watch on.

"During the game we try to check if the fundamentals in terms of organisation and individual behaviour are there," he says. "If we don't break those fundamental principles of the game, then of course, you're checking the strengths of the other team and we try to use our strengths to hit them in the points we believe they're weaker.

"We try to put our best things against the worst things of the other team. We also follow our team very carefully and see that we don't drop from the level we should play at all the time. Sometimes it's not enough for us to win. Manchester United has to win and play good football because playing good football is the guarantee of success."

Should the need for tactical tinkering arise, half time is the ideal time for Sir Alex and the coaches to deliver their amendments to the players.

"At half time you're talking about a matter of minutes, just to try and change the perspective of the players' attitude or the way the game's

Cristiano Ronaldo leaves the fray to a standing ovation from manager and fans alike.

going, or give encouragement," says Phelan. "You might try to discourage them from things they're doing which aren't working and give them alternatives. Sometimes you'll give them loads of information, but on other occasions you give them nothing and let them chill out, relax and leave it at that.

"You have to play the game with them. You don't know what mood they're in, it could depend on the performance, so you have to be particular with what you say – or you don't say anything. You get to know the moods through working with them every day. There are certain times when you would not say a particular thing. Even if you wanted to, you wouldn't because you know you might get a negative rebound off it. So you just bite your lip and walk on eggshells!"

The players return to the fray enlightened and ready to see out the remainder of the 90 minutes, ideally to a positive end. As the goals fly in, as they invariably do, the man who hails each one is stadium announcer Alan Keegan. A lifelong United fan, Alan's job is ever so slightly encumbered by a partisan streak a mile long.

"From a responsibility point of view and trying to be impartial, you try to hold a proper court at pitchside," he says, before grinning. "But if I'm being honest, sometimes the emotions are too much and you just let go. People ask me what my best memory is, and one of them has to be the Roma game [in April 2007]. The team certainly kept me busy that night and it was an absolute pleasure. It was superb just to be part of that emotion, stood at the side of the pitch and sharing the emotion with the backroom staff was fantastic.

"At the end of the day, albeit that I want to be professional, I am a United fan. That goes for when we concede too. You try to put the announcement over in a professional way, but there's bound to be a hint of disappointment. Anybody who follows United and listens to the announcements will understand. I listen to the rest of the announcers around the country and they're the same – it's only natural."

Keegan's working relationship with the Football Association had flourished through covering England games and FA Cup semi-finals at Old Trafford, and paved the way for him to become the voice of Wembley Stadium after its high-profile facelift.

Rather incongruously, however, his career as matchday announcer was conceived at an unlikely starting point.

"The opportunity came up many years ago to work for Manchester City with their Junior Blues scheme," he explains. "Throughout the nine months of the season, the Junior Blues had a meeting once a month where about four or five hundred kids would turn up with parents, and also a group of players would turn up. I got the job of hosting those events so that was always the starting point if you like, my foot in the door of working in football.

"One thing led to another and the club wanted me to do some on-pitch stuff promoting the Junior Blues, this was pre-match before the main announcer. Whenever he was off I'd fill in for him, so that's where I started getting into the role of matchday announcer and I absolutely loved it.

"I joined United the year after the Treble. When the opportunity came up it was absolutely brilliant. I was still working with City, but I'd also started working with United in the corporate hospitality suites two seasons before. It was like a double life. To then become the announcer at Old Trafford was just a dream come true, and part of the condition was that I left City. I've never let go of my season tickets in the Stretford End, I've held on to them till now so my family have them.

"In fact, the wage at City was a pair of season tickets at Maine Road! The reason I always enjoyed the job was that I was guaranteed a pair of derby tickets, even if it meant sitting with the City fans."

Alan's role of unofficial cheerleader has gathered weight and momentum down the years, with Sir Alex open in his desire to see the fans whipped up into a frenzy in order to fire up the players.

"I think it's important," says Keegan. "I know it's been said by Sir Alex in the media, and he's come to me and said 'just go for it'. Enjoy it and put it over to the fans so that they can be the twelfth man. It's a great position to be in. Not that we need geeing up, but sometimes you do need that 'come on let's go for it'. It can make a difference.

"Every football fan knows what I'm doing. Nobody likes being told what to do, but I think they understand they can make a difference, as they did at certain times during the title-winning 2006/07 season. That's the whole idea. We're all behind the club and we try to get as much of a positive reaction as we can at whatever level, whether you're kicking a ball on the field or a fan in the stand just getting behind the team. I'm no different. There are days where we need to lift that momentum and help the team. It's part and parcel of being a football fan."

As Keegan announces each goal to the stadium, safety supervisor Arthur Roberts is watching the fall-out and general safety picture unfold from the Old Trafford control room in the south-east corner of the ground, just next to the away fans.

"I never get a chance to sit and watch a game because I'm so busy looking after the safety of everybody inside the stadium," says Roberts. "That said, what happens on the pitch can have a huge impact on what happens in the stands and whenever United score our immediate focus switches to the visiting section to see what their reaction is.

"We're able to view all the car parks, every turnstile, every exit gate, and the concourses via our internal and external CCTV cameras around the ground. We have in excess of a hundred and the external cameras can see as far as the Barton Flyover on the M60 which is several miles away from the stadium. That allows us to monitor the traffic and pedestrian movements prior to and after matches."

17 THE AFTERMATH

Once Alan Keegan has announced the final score and bid a group farewell to the departing masses, it's time for the rest of the matchday workforce to set about returning Old Trafford to its spotless pre-match state.

Tony Sinclair and his ground staff head straight on to the pitch to tend any divots or scarring, and easily spend an hour making repairs. All around them, scrutiny staff begin sweeping and cleaning the seating areas and Tony Strudwick will often put late or unused substitutes through a warm-down consisting of various stretches and running.

Deep within the bowels of the dressing rooms, meanwhile, the

Edwin van der Sar greets fans outside Old Trafford after the final whistle – the players know they will have to pose for photographs and sign autographs wherever they go.

remaining players shower and change, while Sir Alex and his staff prepare to put rivalries aside and invite the visitors for a post-match drink in the manager's office.

"We always invite our opponents in for a drink, and mostly they all come in," says the Reds' boss. "Sometimes a manager can be a bit late because he may be doing his press obligations and things like that, but under normal circumstances most clubs come in. It shouldn't depend on how the game goes."

On their departure from Old Trafford, the players will take time out to sign autographs for the hordes of devoted fans who wait outside the ground.

"Of course it's mad," says Ole Gunnar Solskjaer, talking about the near-deification bestowed upon modern footballers. "We're good at playing football, there are so many other people out there who are good at other things. It's that celebrity thing that I don't really understand about football. Everyone can relate to football and more or less everyone likes it, so I understand that there's such a huge fan base.

"You get a different view when you see someone on the television. For me, seeing Bryan Robson and Bobby Charlton on the telly, those were the ones I looked at as proper legends. That's just the way it is. When you see someone from a distance you create your own different perception of them."

"When I was younger I waited outside Goodison [Park] and Everton's training ground for autographs," adds Wayne Rooney. "And when you see kids waiting now, that's why you always try to make time and sign autographs for them. I remember when I was younger, a few players walked past [and didn't sign] so I know how it feels. So you try and do it as much as you can."

Back inside the stadium, Arthur Roberts meets with the police, stewards and medical services for a debriefing, while over in the dressing room the clean-up operation continues as the coaching staff clear away their equipment in readiness for the next game.

"The day after a match we'll head straight to Old Trafford for about 8 a.m. to collect the rest of the kit to be washed," says kit manager Albert Morgan. "I then start organising the kit for training that morning and look ahead to the next game. I couldn't do it without my staff. I've got fantastic staff. Everyone works very hard, but it all comes back to the fact that it's like being part of a family at this club.

"The demands can be enormous sometimes, but you just get on with it because you're all working towards the same thing. You're like a little hamster in the wheel – you're at it all the time – when one game has ended, it's on to the next."

United's twelfth man:
the Red Army.

Part Five

REDS ON THE ROAD

"The fans give us so much inspiration, especially away from home. The buzz you get from hearing them sing your name is amazing. That'll never change. When you hear the supporters buzzing, you know they're up for it and we've got to be up for it as well."

JOHN O'SHEA

DOMESTIC MATTERS

18

Continuity and routine are key aspects of the preparation undertaken for United's away games. Almost without exception, the Reds go through the same routine for every domestic away fixture. After a light training session at Carrington the day before a game, the players and coaching staff regroup later that afternoon and head to their designated base for the next 24 hours.

"We always stay over in a hotel the night before an away match, even if we're playing a local team," reveals Darren Fletcher. "We usually go straight up to our rooms when we first arrive – we all have our own rooms – and then sit down for dinner at about seven o'clock.

John O'Shea, Wayne Rooney and Wes Brown entertain themselves on the coach to a match.

"After that, a few of us will usually play a few games on the PlayStation, before heading off to bed anywhere between nine and eleven. Of course, the next day's game is on your mind but I've always been a good sleeper so it doesn't keep me awake all the night."

Some members of the Reds' coaching staff had no such luck when United were preparing for a match at Sunderland in October 2005. The away trips often allow for horseplay among the coaching staff, with chief prankster Tony Coton the instigator in this particular tale.

"We were staying at Lumley Castle around Halloween time," he recalls. "It's not like your average hotel – all the staff wear medieval garb and it's definitely haunted so the lads don't like staying there much. Before the trip, myself and Mick Phelan had bought a few horror masks and a couple of walkie-talkies from a joke shop to take with us. I knew the manager of the hotel from my days at Sunderland and managed to wangle a pass key for all the rooms off him.

"First we went to Albert's [Morgan] room and put a skull in his bed. We then headed to Valter's [di Salvo, the former fitness coach] room and put a walkie-talkie underneath his. Everyone gets a teddy bear in their rooms at this particular hotel and we made sure we put Valter's next to his bed. Later on when he had gone up to his room, Mick and I put the masks on and went and knocked on his door. We hid before he answered and then got the other walkie-talkie and started talking in a spooky voice. This carried on for a while.

"Carlos [Queiroz] opened his door a bit because he could hear us laughing. He couldn't see us at first but when Mick and I poked our heads around the corner with our masks on we almost had to scrape him off the ceiling! Albert was also in on the joke but he got the shock of his life when he pulled his sheets back to find the skull in his bed!

"The next morning when we were having breakfast Valter walked in, white as a sheet, looking as if he'd hardly had any sleep. We asked him if he was okay and he told us he'd had a very bad night. He then said that the teddy bear in his room had been talking to him! We were killing ourselves laughing by this point and had to come clean. He took it very well in fairness and thought it was a good joke."

The jokes are put on hold when matchday finally comes around. Kick-off times dictate the players' pre-game routine but they always have their pre-match meal three hours before, be it morning, noon or night.

"My matchday routine is set in stone," reveals skipper Gary Neville. "I've done the same thing for every game for the last fifteen years or so. I always come down early for the pre-match meal and more often than not I have spaghetti and tomato sauce with some bread. I then make my way to the coach – I always sit in the same seat – twenty minutes or so before I'm supposed to be there. We all get ready for games in different ways – some of the lads will come down for their pre-match meal just as it's being served and will stay in the dining room chatting until we leave. I don't talk a great deal before games and like being on my own to prepare myself."

The coach journey to the stadium can last for up to 30 minutes, after which the players focus their energy on preparing for kick-off.

"Once you get to the ground everyone goes into their own matchday mode," says Darren Fletcher. "It's important to try and relax before the game but there are usually lots of things running through your head, such as where you should be at set-pieces and which players you'll be up against. A few of the lads have pre-match rituals and routines, but I personally try and stay away from superstitions because they can take over your life!"

"I've done all sorts of things down the years in the build-up to matches," adds Rio Ferdinand. "I used to put strapping on a certain foot in a certain way at a certain time, and I also used to wear a ring on my little finger for good luck. As soon as I walk out on to the pitch and hit the white line, the one thing I always do is jump! I've no idea where it came from, it's just a superstition which has always stayed with me."

"Everyone prepares differently," chips in Nemanja Vidic. "Some players like to play music, others like to joke around; Ronny [Cristiano Ronaldo] always likes to have a laugh no matter who we're playing! But me, I like to concentrate. I might juggle the ball around in the dressing room for a little bit, but I usually stay quite quiet so I can focus my mind. It's one of those things that stays with you from a youngster. I still prepare for matches in the same way I did when I was a young boy."

A domestic away trip will inevitably throw up a return to a former club for some individuals. Rio Ferdinand, a product of the West Ham United youth system before switching to Elland Road, has endured such

The team bus is ready to take the players to an evening match.

an experience but he believes it's a challenge players relish.

"You always want to do well when you go back to face your old team, it's a natural instinct," he insists. "I always get a great reception whenever I go back to West Ham, I've still got a good rapport with the fans at Upton Park. Leeds is the other side of the coin though. The huge rivalry between United and Leeds means they don't like me much there!"

The players do not find out who has made the starting eleven until an hour and a half before kick-off when Sir Alex conducts his all-important team-talk.

"The manager provides us with information about the opposition and discusses their strengths and weaknesses as well," explains Fletcher. "He'll talk to us about what he wants us to do to counter those factors and focuses on the best ways of getting the result we need. He'll then name the team.

"We don't find out who's in until then because if you knew you weren't in the side the day before the game you might not be as focused as you should be. This way it means everyone is prepared in the right way. If you're in then great, but if you're not, you quickly get over your disappointment and wish the rest of the lads good luck. The last thing the manager always says to us is go out and enjoy yourselves."

"It's important to hear him say that because in the high pressure games it's sometimes difficult to get into the game and enjoy it," adds Wayne Rooney. "He expects us to give one hundred per cent and that's what all the players do. We understand that it's our job to do that and we all want to play and win for him."

Some of the more experienced campaigners will occasionally voice their own suggestions at how best to combat the opposition.

"The likes of Ryan [Giggs] and Gary [Neville] will at times go round and have a little chat with some of the lads – they're great like that," says Fletcher. "Even if they're not involved, they'll come into the dressing room and have a little word if they feel they need to."

"There are occasions when I'll pick out certain things concerning the defenders," adds Reds captain Neville. "And if I feel there is something very important that needs saying to one of the midfielders or the strikers, I'll say it."

"Players like Gary, Ryan and Scholesy have been there and done it and gained so much experience over the years," continues Fletcher. "It's great that they are able to pass on some words of encouragement."

Once the whistle blows, there is nothing more that Sir Alex and his coaching staff can do. While most managers watch the action unfold from the bench, the United boss tends to favour the view from a loftier perch during the first 45 minutes.

"Alex usually sits next to me for the first half of away games," reveals chief executive David Gill. "He's up there to observe the match from a different perspective and he goes through a fair few packets of chewing gum! He always goes down to the dug-out just before half time, or earlier if things aren't going according to plan."

The United manager isn't the only one to turn to Wrigley's finest when it comes to watching from the sidelines.

"I get through a good few packets when I'm on the bench because I get so nervous," admits Fletcher. "You kick every ball when you're sat there and I usually have no fingernails left by the end of most games! I think you're more vocal when you're on the bench, especially if you are warming up and the linesman, who might be stood next to you, gives a poor decision. You're more like a fan when you're on the bench."

For the majority of Premier League clubs, the visit of United represents their biggest test of the campaign and for some lesser sides it equates to their seasonal cup final. It's a scenario which comes with the territory of playing for the Reds and it's something the whole team seems to thrive on.

"I relish the pressure that comes with every team wanting to beat United," insists Vidic. "It's actually something I'm quite used to. When I was at Red Star Belgrade everyone wanted to beat us because they are the biggest club in Serbia. It was the same at Spartak Moscow and of course, now at United. The most important thing is having the mentality that you always need to win."

The satisfaction that comes from netting victories over both title and local rivals is second to none. And those in the big games represent the biggest coups.

"The Liverpool match is the one we all look forward to," declares Sir Alex. "I think it's the right atmosphere and it's a fantastic challenge for us. Games there are never easy; you're always on a knife edge with those kinds of matches."

"You always want to win every game you play but those against the likes of Liverpool and Chelsea are the big ones and you desperately want to beat them," continues Vidic. "For me, the Serbia versus Bosnia international match has the same effect.

"United versus Liverpool is a big game throughout Europe. It's the equivalent of Madrid versus Barcelona or one of the big derbies in Italy. When I first joined the club, of course, I knew United versus Liverpool was a massive game, but it takes time for you to really feel the club within you. When I was at Belgrade it was easy because I've supported them all my life and they are in my heart. But now I feel the passion that surrounds the Liverpool game myself and I know how important it is for the fans, the players and everyone at Old Trafford. I didn't understand that passion the first time I played against them. I began to realise it in the second match and then in the third game I played, when John O'Shea scored the winner in the last minute [in March 2007], I really felt it and it was a great feeling to beat them."

Rewind to Sheasy's big day: Saturday 3 March 2007 on a sunny afternoon at Anfield: Cristiano Ronaldo is stood poised over a free kick in dangerous territory. As the clock ticks past the 92nd minute mark, United players jostle for positions inside the area as the Kop looks on. Despite having played the last four minutes with ten men, the Reds remain on level terms at 0-0. But they have a chance, a big chance to change that scoreline in their favour and steal the points that can have a huge say on the destination of the 2006–07 Premiership title. The ball is whipped in …

Rewind to the 71st minute and a crunching tackle from Jamie Carragher on Wayne Rooney. It's a major blow for the Reds – the gaping hole in Rooney's right thigh needs stitches and substitute John O'Shea is summoned from the bench. The Irish international, and indeed former Liverpool fan, remembers the drama unfold like it was yesterday, but even he couldn't have dreamt what was to follow …

14:16 – 73 mins: "I was warming up on the touchline and the next thing I knew Albert came running over, arms flailing in the air as usual, yelling 'You're coming on, you're coming on!' I didn't actually see Carragher's tackle on Wayne, but I didn't think it was too bad because Wayne did his best not to show he was hurt. Being a former Evertonian the last thing he would have wanted was to come off at Anfield – he would have tried to carry on even if he had two broken legs! But obviously Wayne couldn't carry on so I came on.

14:29 – 86 mins: "I'd only been on the pitch just over ten minutes when Scholesy got sent off. We knew we couldn't lose the game and at that point we were just thinking let's hang on and get a draw.

14:35 – 90 mins (+2): "Giggsy did brilliantly to win a free kick down the left, near the edge of the area. He held off a couple of players but got pushed in the back by Steve Finnan. I'm not sure Liverpool were too happy about the award but it was definitely a foul. Ronaldo was stood over it and I remember thinking I should go and stand near the

Rio Ferdinand is the only player quick enough to catch John O'Shea after he scores an injury time winner in front of the Kop.

Opposite: Players and fans rejoice after a monumental win.

goalkeeper because any little nick on the ball could take it in. The way Ronny whips the ball in when he goes for goal makes it very hard for keepers. Louis [Saha] made a great run across Pepe Reina and he was very unlucky not to score, but he still put the keeper off and fortunately I took a gamble. Normally I run round the back post, but this time I went to the front post and when the ball dropped to me I managed to tuck it away into the roof of the net.

"My first instinct was to run towards the United fans at the other end of the ground. All the lads were shattered and couldn't keep up with me, although Rio eventually managed to catch up! My brother had come over for the game from Ireland and he was in with the United supporters as well. I remember looking around and seeing virtually the

whole ground just stood stationary except for the away section. People were jumping about everywhere and falling all over the place; it was a great feeling to see the fans so happy. Over the years a lot of people have made it known I was a Liverpool fan when I was younger, but I can definitely say that's changed now! Gary Neville said to me in the dressing room afterwards that I'd just realised his dream – scoring the winner against Liverpool in the last minute in front of the Kop. I've got a framed picture of the moment on my wall in my house. It's something I'll never forget and hopefully I can do it a few more times in my career."

That sentiment is felt just as ardently by United fans everywhere, particularly those who follow the team home and away. An Anfield scalp is always top of any Red's wish list, and the supporters certainly play their part in helping the team achieve success on the road.

"They give us so much inspiration, especially away from home," says O'Shea. "The buzz you get from hearing them sing your name is amazing. That'll never change. When you hear the fans buzzing, even in the warm-up sometimes, you know they're up for it and we've got to be up for it as well. It feeds through to the team and makes you want to play well for them."

A TASTE OF THE CONTINENT

19

"**F**light MON 9330 to Lille is now ready for boarding," declares the Tannoy announcer at Manchester Airport. It's 10 a.m. on Monday morning, the day before the Reds' last 16, first leg clash with the French side at Lens' Stade Felix Bollaert, and Sir Alex Ferguson and his players are preparing to embark on their latest 2006/07 Champions League mission.

The travelling party, which also includes the backroom staff of coaches, club doctor, physiotherapist, kit manager and masseur, are not

The players getting ready for another trip to Europe.

alone on their chartered flight to France. In keeping with previous trips, club directors and staff representing United's media and marketing departments are also in attendance. Club sponsors and their guests are on board as well, as are the British press, who are situated at the rear of the plane.

Two other key figures on the trip are club secretary Ken Ramsden and Travelcare Sports operations manager Phil Morris who coordinates all of United's European excursions on behalf of the club. This will be the pair's second expedition to Lille having completed their customary reconnaissance trip two weeks earlier.

"We take representatives from Greater Manchester Police and the FA's safety adviser with us and meet with the British Embassy or Consular staff in the city where we're due to play," explains Ramsden who relays his findings to United's coaching and medical staff. "We'll find a suitable hotel for the team to stay in, go to the ground, check out the facilities and meet with the host club and negotiate team colours, arrival times, training times and so forth.

"We also look at things from the fans' perspective so we're able to tell them a bit more about the trip and also warn them if they need to beware of anything. I think the supporters sometimes get frustrated when they go to a venue and think it isn't up to standard. They wonder why we haven't done anything about it, but we can't unfortunately. We can't say to UEFA we're not going to play a match because the opposition's stadium is not very clean or the toilets aren't up to standard. You wish you could sometimes because what United fans encounter on occasion is pretty poor in some venues. All we can do is make representations."

Despite what some supporters may believe, the club go to extreme lengths to ensure travelling Reds are treated with respect.

"Before we were due to play a match in France some years ago, we found that there were no toilets for our fans to use," adds Ken. "We complained to the host club but they wouldn't do anything about it, so we ended up having to pay for a number of portable loos to be brought into our section."

Ken and Phil also keep club doctor Steve McNally abreast of their findings to ensure the club's medical team have cover for all eventualities.

"I will often get calls from them when they are visiting the stadium and hotel filling me in on the facilities available to us," explains Steve. "If something isn't right, it allows us to make any requests well in advance of our trip or make arrangements to take any extra kit we may need."

On arrival at Lille Airport just after 11 a.m., following a 70-minute flight, the travelling party head to their hotel for some lunch while the press are transported to their own, separate hotel. Afterwards Sir Alex and defender Patrice Evra hold a pre-match press conference in front of the world's media. The players spend the remainder of the afternoon resting in their rooms, before returning to their private dining area for a light snack around 4.30 p.m.

An evening training session is next on the agenda, although unusually this takes place at Lens' Le Gaillette training ground amid concerns over the pitch at the Stade Felix Bollaert. Lille's Metropole Stadium does

Sir Alex and Patrice Evra give a press conference ahead of the game against Lille in February 2007.

Everything is made ready for the practice session in Lens.

There's still time for a joke between Sir Alex and Louis Saha in practice; the serious work begins the next day.

not meet UEFA requirements which is why the match has been switched to neighbours Lens' ground. The Reds will typically train at the opposition's home stadium the night prior to a Champions League game, before returning to their hotel for dinner and an early night.

"That's the general routine we follow," says John O'Shea, "but we've changed it around a few times as well. Instead of flying off in the morning the day before the game and then training at the opposition's ground later that afternoon, we've trained at Carrington first thing then flown out and relaxed for the rest of the day. The lads don't mind which way we do it, it's just a case of the manager and coaching staff working out which option benefits us best."

"We never see much of the places we go to," adds Ole Gunnar Solskjaer. "Everyone thinks that footballers have seen so much of the world, but in actual fact all you really see are hotel rooms, airports and stadiums."

No matter which part of Europe they visit, the team always stick to the UK time zone so there is minimal disruption to their pre-match routine. Ensuring the players stay relaxed and in the right frame of mind ahead of a game is of paramount importance to Sir Alex and his coaching staff.

"European trips are always a bit tense especially as every one of our Champions League matches always receives big media coverage," admits the manager. "We've enjoyed mixed fortunes down the years, but there's no question we should have won the European Cup more times than we have done. Some years we've been unlucky, other times we've thrown it away or just haven't been good enough. The trips can be quite hard going, but it's all about getting the players ready physically and mentally and also making sure they relax in the build-up to games."

That form of relaxation – if it can be deemed as such – often comes in the shape of a players v coaching staff quiz. Hosted by club photographer John Peters, with assistance from son and fellow club snapper Matt, the quiz is broken up into different rounds on various subjects ranging from Scottish history (Sir Alex's favourite) to TV soaps (a popular category with the players). It's a contest that neither side likes to lose.

"For a long time we were battering the players but now it's getting more even because the quiz-master is on their side," jokes Sir Alex. "They've got John in their pocket! He asks questions on soap operas and all those anoraks sit and watch them every night! They can tell their actors and actresses from shows like *Hollyoaks* and all the rest of it, but we're a bit more mature when it comes to that sort of thing. John does get battered though, he gets all sorts of abuse!"

"I've had a few bread rolls and tomatoes thrown my way by the losing side in the past!" reveals quiz-master John Peters. "Ryan [Giggs] always does quite well and, when he was here, Nicky Butt used to pull answers out from nowhere!"

"The quizzes are normally pretty close although I think the staff won the last one," adds John O'Shea. "But they've got a secret weapon in the Doc – he came out with some great answers for them. Wayne always does pretty well for us. He's a bit like Nicky Butt used to be, Butty would come out with some great guesses. It's a great bit of fun and it helps to relax you before the game. Sometimes though it can go a bit far and it has been known for fruit wars to be started with bananas and oranges being flung at each other. Obviously no one hits the manager though!"

Mike Phelan echoes Sir Alex's sentiments, insisting the players have an unfair advantage because of their affinity with the quiz-master.

"John sets the rules out and then changes them when the players decide to change things," insists Phelan. "All the players know the

Sir Alex chats to P Diddy the day before the match in Copenhagen in November 2006.

modern music questions whereas we and the manager don't have a clue. But then we're pretty good on history and things like that. Giggsy's pretty sharp, but all the players are actually very good at guessing. You wonder how they know things sometimes, but somehow they get around it and come up with the answers. For us, all the medical team are brainboxes. They're all university graduates and very clued up. Us coaches don't know anything about that! Things can become very competitive and the quiz can last anything from an hour to three hours, it just depends on who's winning!"

Special visits from celebrity fans have been known to take place during some European trips. Simply Red front man Mick Hucknall, a personal friend of Sir Alex's, has called in to the team hotel in the past, while US entertainment mogul P Diddy stopped off at the Reds' HQ during their trip to Copenhagen in November 2006. The rap superstar was in town for the MTV Europe Music Awards and he was keen to meet up with old pals Rio Ferdinand and Wayne Rooney, who paid a substantial sum of money during a charity auction at the Beckhams' pre-World Cup charity party in May 2006 to spend the weekend at Diddy's New York mansion. Diddy, who was presented with a United shirt by the team, also got the chance to meet Sir Alex for the first time.

"The manager didn't have a clue who he was or what he did!" laughs Rio. "I admire him greatly – he's a very successful person who has come from not very much. He's built a massive empire that's worth millions of pounds around so many different things – his record label, his clothing range and even his own fragrance – you have to admire that. He doesn't know too much about football but he's learning!"

"He's a great guy," adds Rooney. "I grew up listening to his music and it's weird to have the chance to meet."

A handful of the players like to warm up for their looming on-field battle with a supposedly friendly round of PSP warfare. Formerly devotees of Pro Evolution Soccer, the septet of Darren Fletcher, Wes Brown, John O'Shea, Nemanja Vidic, Wayne Rooney, Michael Carrick and Rio Ferdinand have turned their attentions to a new PlayStation genre.

Introduced to the squad by United starlets Jonny Evans and Darron Gibson during the 2006 pre-season tour to South Africa, SOCOM is an army game which sees US Navy SEALS come face-to-face with Mercenaries in a traditional good against evil yarn. The SEALS are armed with a better arsenal, naturally, while the Mercenaries have to adopt more sophisticated tactics and cunning as a result.

An original line-up of four against four saw Fletcher, Brown, O'Shea and Vidic do battle – literally – with Rooney, Carrick, Ferdinand and former Reds winger Richardson.

According to Fletcher, a contest that initially started out as a bit of fun has since progressed to a much more serious level.

"We've all become addicted to SOCOM," he admits. "And it's got to a highly tactical level now. Rio is particularly tactical. He never likes to come out into the open and get involved in a shoot-off. He tends to keep his team in a little bunker so when you venture out into the open he's ready with his rockets to shoot you! We're by far the best team, that's why Rio has had to resort to his caveman tactics of sitting in a bunker!"

Ferdinand strongly disagrees with the Scot's analysis of his strategy, insisting his side have the edge.

"Our team is definitely the best," he declares. "Me, Wazza and Michael regularly bury Vida, Wes, Sheasy and Fletch. They're not on the same wavelength as us. The only time they ever really beat us is when thay have more players than us which happens when one or two of the lads are injured and don't travel. And when that's the case they celebrate like they've won the World Cup!

"We also play against the Chelsea lads when we're away with England," adds Rio. "It's pretty even though, sometimes we win and other times they do."

"The games are always very close, but our team usually does okay," says Vidic. "Sheasy and Wes are a good players, but Rio always hides in bunkers and waits with his grenades so he can shoot us. He's a real coward!"

Such is the impact that SOCOM has had on the players, they've even based some of their goal celebrations around the combative action, and the rivalry between the two sides even continues out of hours.

"Some of our wives and girlfriends are unhappy with us because we play at home online too!" reveals John O'Shea.

"We all think SOCOM is the best game ever invented! We get a bit loud sometimes when we're travelling away and some people aren't too happy with us. I won't name names but we know we have to be a bit quieter! It's all about the winning attitude that we have around the club – everyone wants to do well at whatever they do.

"It's swings and roundabouts which team are on top," adds the Irishman. "But that could all change now following Wazza's transfer to my team. It was Wayne's decision – he wanted to leave Rio's team and join mine. He's been given a trial period so we'll wait and see what happens from that!"

Rooney's explanation for his decision is simple: "The other team was full of individuals, Sheasy's lot play as a team," he smiles.

Predictably, Rooney's former team-mate Michael Carrick sees the shift of allegiance in a different light, and believes Rio and Co. are bene-fiting from the striker's departure, which he insists was a group decision.

"We kicked Wazza off our team – he was shocking!" insists the

England midfielder. "We brought him up – me, Rio and Kieran when he was here – Wazza started playing with us. We groomed him through the academy and then packed him off to the other team. Since then they've been shocking. We've been working them!"

According to O'Shea the two teams might soon have other challengers to contend with.

"Patrice [Evra] and Louis [Saha] are still quite into Pro Evolution Soccer but we're slowly converting them to SOCOM," he explains. "Louis in particular is getting into it but they're not near our standards yet. We're not sure if we can afford to coach them though as it could have detrimental effects on us!"

"We play a lot of Pro Evo," chips in Saha. "Patrice reckons he is the best but he's always going to say that! I'm very humble so I wouldn't actually say that I'm the best, but I'm not bad. It changes all the time. I remember beating Patrice 6-0 on one occasion but he somehow still

Team-mates on and off the pitch: Darren Fletcher and John O'Shea go to war together on the PSP.

managed to get to the final and beat Ji [-sung Park]. But Ji wasn't allowed to play his proper team, so it wasn't fair. It was controversial! The tournaments are another good example of the squad spirit. We all have a good laugh together."

The day of the game is all about preparing for kick-off. Aside from the players themselves, there is also a big responsibility on United's backroom staff, not least Albert Morgan.

"European trips are very different to domestic away games because we have to take all the training kit with us on top of the matchday stuff," he explains. "You also have to make sure things are in a certain place at the right time. I usually get given a suite at our hotel so there is room for the kit as well. All the furniture is removed from the living area so I can spread everything out. I still worry about things and there has been many a time when I've woken up in the middle of the night wondering if I've forgotten something! On the odd occasion something has been left behind but I've always managed to sort it out."

As ever, being on the road gives idle hands the chance to make mischief. European away games are often a source of much mirth for the backroom staff, with everyone keen to dish out the japes.

"I always remember the gaffer playing a trick on me when we played in Monaco one time," recalls Albert. "I'd cleaned all the players' boots and left them out to dry on my balcony. The boss got a TV crew to move them all round the corner so I couldn't see them and then came in and said he'd just seen some kids climb onto the balcony and pinch all the boots. I ran outside and saw they'd gone so I jumped over the wall and ran like mad to try and catch the culprits. When I turned around everyone was stood on the balcony laughing hysterically and, of course, the boots were all there!"

After Tony Strudwick has put the squad through a mid-morning stretching session, the players will watch a specially prepared video on the opposition. They are then free to do as they please: the majority opt to return to their rooms for an afternoon nap. The squad reconvenes around 5.30 p.m. for Sir Alex's team meeting during which he names his starting line-up.

"The build-up to the match is all about resting and saving your energy," says Ole Gunnar Solskjaer. "The stretching session gets your body going and we also do a light jog with quick feet patterns. It's something that we've started doing over the last three or four years. After lunch some of us might go for a walk within the grounds of our hotel or just rest in our rooms, before we sit down for the team meeting."

As with all games, the players have their pre-match meal three hours before kick-off. A police escort to the stadium ensures they arrive at the Stade Felix Bollaert around an hour and a quarter before kick-off.

A number of the Reds' backroom staff are ready and waiting upon the team's entrance into the dressing room having travelled down to the ground a little earlier to prepare the area and set up a temporary medical station.

"The players will come and see me, Steve [McNally] or Garry [Armer] and start having their strappings, stretches or any manual treatments in preparation for the warm-up," explains head physiotherapist Rob Swire. "Some of them have specific routines they like to go through ahead of kick-off. While they're warming up outside, I'll get bits and pieces ready like bags of ice and make sure my 'running-on' bag is sorted.

"I'm always there if the players want to come and find me. I don't go around checking all of them every minute of the day, because constantly checking them can put doubts in their minds. If they've got a problem they'll come to me. Once they return to the dressing room after the warm-up, we'll do some last minute preparations before they go out for the match."

Away from the action on the pitch the club spends much time and energy overseeing plans for the safe transportation of United fans, who are travelling on official club trips, to and from the ground.

"We have an organisational meeting on the morning of every Champions League game," explains Ken Ramsden. "It's attended by representatives from both clubs, as well as the referees and a UEFA official. We go through everything surrounding the game, including what transport provisions there are for our fans after the match. Some people may say that's not our concern, but it is. They're our fans."

The well documented crowd trouble during the 2006/07 away trips against Lille and Roma were a major concern for the club and the game

Paul Scholes leaves
the team's hotel to
head off to a game.

as a whole, and the heavy-handed tactics of the local police in Italy even prompted an investigation by the Home Office.

"Rightly or wrongly English fans have got a reputation for bad behaviour," admits Ramsden. "When we go over to meet with the opposition club's officials we always reiterate the point that our fans are not coming over to cause trouble. Treat them respectfully and they'll behave respectfully. But the problem we have is cultures in different countries vary, and policing styles can be very different. We can say that's wrong but that's what happens in some places. It's nothing to do with English football fans or United, it's to do with the culture of that particular country."

The usual procedure at the final whistle is to keep visiting Reds locked inside the ground to give opposition supporters time to disperse, hopefully ensuring that there are no clashes between the two sets of fans. Back in the dressing room, a handful of players will be required to provide a urine sample as part of the doping regulations in force within the game.

"It takes place unannounced at some matches and it's a random selection when it comes to which players take the test," explains Steve

McNally. "The team doctors do the draw for domestic games at half time, but they always draw for the opposing team. For European matches, the UEFA control officer does the draw in the seventy-fifth minute of the match in the presence of a club representative. I'm usually not there for that draw because I'm sat on the bench. It's then my responsibility to make sure the players report to the doping station straight after the final whistle and do not go to the dressing room first."

Once that procedure is complete the players must then scramble their way through the bear garden that is the "mixed zone" – a term used to describe the gathering of every media correspondent attending the

Ronaldo, Scholes, Saha and Rooney do their pre-match exercises.

United fans get ready to
watch the Reds take on Lille.

Cristiano Ronaldo
runs the gauntlet of
the mixed zone.

game within the confines of the players' tunnel. Under UEFA rules each member from both teams who has played a part in a Champions League match must walk through the mixed zone on their way out of the stadium. As they pass through the crowded area the press, who usually split up into groups – daily papers, Sunday papers and TV crews – so as to keep their content exclusive to their own section of the media, will ask specific players for their reaction to the game. It is entirely up to the players themselves whether or not they stop to talk. Given the excellent result in France, thanks to Ryan Giggs' late winner and the controversy that followed after some of the Lille players threatened to walk off the pitch in protest at the Welshman's quick-thinking, there is much to discuss.

The Reds will, on occasion, prolong their stay in a particular destination before flying direct to Manchester or a particular city where their next game is scheduled to take place, but in general they usually fly straight back after the final whistle, arriving home anywhere between 1 and 2 a.m. A light training session follows a few hours later at Carrington, before it's time to focus on the next challenge that lies ahead.

20

WEMBLEY WEEK

May 2007. After a seven-year absence the FA Cup final, the most famous domestic cup competition in the world, returns to its rightful home, Wembley Stadium. Fittingly its most successful club are there too, appearing in their eighth FA Cup final under Sir Alex Ferguson.

The Reds, who have won the competition a record 11 times, earned their cup final berth the hard way having overcome Premiership opposition in every round. Now another top-flight team – and main title rivals – stand in United's way as they go in search of a fourth domestic double at the redeveloped 90,000-capacity Wembley Stadium.

United return
to Wembley.

Nemanja Vidic gets measured up for his FA Cup final suit.

In a game billed as the "dream final", United face a Chelsea side (who won the last cup final at the old Wembley in May 2000) desperate for revenge having seen the Reds regain the Premiership crown and in turn deny them a hat-trick of title victories. Sir Alex's men are equally as determined for victory after losing out in a penalty shoot-out to Arsenal in the 2005 final despite dominating the game.

Ahead of the competition's 126th final, the Reds get measured up for their traditional cup final suits and take part in a special media open day at Carrington. They may have eased their foot off the pedal in their final two Premiership games, having already been assured of the title a few days earlier, but, come Wembley week, the whole squad are fully focused on ensuring there is a successful finale to the historic occasion that lies in wait …

MONDAY 14 MAY

Carrington is buzzing. Yesterday, after a four-year absence, the Reds were presented with their ninth Premiership title, and not even the Manchester rain or the 1-0 defeat to West Ham could dampen anyone's spirits, especially Wayne Rooney who tasted title glory for the first time in his career.

Designer William Hunt
lines up with his
beloved Reds.

"There's no greater feeling out there," he admits. "I'm absolutely delighted. It's really hard to explain – I can't put it into words, it's unbelievable. It's a massive tournament for us to win. We've had thirty-eight tough games, so to come out on top of that is great for us. Hopefully we won't have to wait another four years to win it again. We can't go too far with our celebrations though because we have to make sure we're ready for the cup final on Saturday."

Injured skipper Gary Neville, who lifted the Premiership trophy aloft with record title-winner Ryan Giggs, is equally proud of the team's achievements, but looks unlikely to play any part in Saturday's Wembley showpiece. "I hope I'll be able to be involved but I'm not sure at the moment," he admits. "I'll be at Wembley whatever though, whether it's in a playing capacity or as a fan. We've had a great few days, but the focus at United is always to move on and we have to think about winning the cup final and make it a really special season."

TUESDAY 15 MAY

After a light training session the players line up outside the Carrington reception for an official photograph in their cup final suits. Designed by renowned Savile Row-based tailor and United fan William Hunt, the navy suits are a popular choice among the players. Hunt has created everything – from the shirts, to the shoes, to the cufflinks. Around 40 suits have been custom-made especially for United's cup final party, which includes the manager and coaching staff. Hunt himself is at Carrington today to double check some final measurements, before he poses alongside his heroes for what will no doubt be a treasured memento.

WEDNESDAY 16 MAY

Ahead of the team's morning training session, Sir Alex holds a pre-match cup final press conference in Carrington's Academy building in front of the world's media. First on the agenda is the injury situation. Aside from long-term absentees Ji-sung Park and Mikael Silvestre, everyone is fit, apart from Louis Saha and Gary Neville. Saha is out with a knee injury, while the United boss confirms his skipper has undergone an operation on his damaged ankle ligaments and is definitely out of the final. In his absence, Ryan Giggs will captain the side as he looks to win a record fifth winners' medal.

"Ryan will be captain and it completes a marvellous season for the lad," insists Sir Alex. "The contribution he has made to us since he joined has been amazing. Hopefully he has a very successful day on Saturday, but regardless of what happens, he stands high [in the list of United legends]. The number of games he has played alone says that. For the last fifteen or sixteen years he has been going up and down that wing, and there is no player who has done that in the Premiership. It's unbelievable."

After training, a number of the players make their way over to face a press grilling. As is normal for a media open day, the radio stations and press agencies are grouped together, as are the daily newspapers; each are assigned two players. The former collude to interview Wes Brown and Nemanja Vidic, while the latter speak to Paul Scholes and John

Wayne Rooney, Kieran Richardson and Wes Brown relax in the grounds.

Oakley Court Hotel in Windsor, United's cup final base.

O'Shea. The television crews, meanwhile, set up within the indoor pitch and grab a word with one or more of the eight players, including Rio Ferdinand, Ole Gunnar Solskjaer and Darren Fletcher, who are earmarked to face the TV cameras. The BBC and Sky – the main rights holders for the final – speak to Wayne Rooney and Cristiano Ronaldo over in the main Carrington building.

THURSDAY 17 MAY

After a morning training session at Carrington, the Reds board a 3 p.m. flight to Heathrow, before heading to their cup final base in Windsor. The team are staying among the tranquil surroundings of Oakley Court Hotel, the place where they stayed before their cup triumphs in 1994, 1996 and 1999.

"We like to take the players away a couple of days before the final so they can properly focus on the game," explains Sir Alex. "I know from experience that as the match draws nearer everyone is pestering you for tickets! So we wanted to get them away from everything so they can relax and prepare for the final in the right way."

Built more than 130 years ago, Oakley Court is one of the most popular and elegant country house hotels in the South East of England. Set in 35 acres of landscaped gardens with lawns that wander gently down to the banks of the River Thames, the Victorian gothic country

The day before the final, and the players train in the morning at Bisham Abbey.

house has proved to be a lucky retreat for the Reds over the years. "We've got good memories of staying here and it's good to be back," says Ryan Giggs. "Hopefully that'll be the case this time round as well."

After an early dinner around 7 p.m., the majority of the players retire to their rooms. But it's a big night for Cristiano Ronaldo who is on his way to collect yet another personal award – the Football Writers' Player of the Year accolade – to mark his tremendous season for the Reds. Ronaldo, along with Sir Alex and assistant manager Carlos Queiroz, are all attending tonight's Football Writers' Dinner at the Royal Lancaster Hotel in central London. Once the awards ceremony is completed, the United trio head back to Windsor to continue their preparations for Saturday.

FRIDAY 18 MAY

After an early breakfast the players travel the short distance to Bisham Abbey, the England team's former training ground, for a morning training session. There's a positive atmosphere among the camp with everyone determined to end the season on a victorious note.

"I've been thinking about the final every day this week and having a

few sleepless nights," admits Wayne Rooney, who experienced the heart-break of defeat against Arsenal in 2005. "As a young boy you always dream of playing in an FA Cup final and to be involved in the first one at the new Wembley is a great honour. I'm sure it'll be a great atmosphere and I can't wait to run out in front of all our fans."

The players return to Oakley Court for lunch before enjoying a short boat trip down the Thames. "The manager decided it would be good for us to get some fresh air," says Ryan Giggs. "We're all feeling confident and are very much looking forward to tomorrow's game now."

Ryan Giggs, Gary Neville and Paul Scholes relax on a boat trip down the Thames.

Perhaps they wouldn't have been so calm if they knew who was at the helm.

SATURDAY 19 MAY

Cup final day is finally here. At 9 a.m. the players sit down to a breakfast buffet (prepared by Chelsea fan and executive head chef Darren Kimber), before returning to their rooms to get ready. It's been a tough morning for John O'Shea, Patrice Evra and Alan Smith, who have been informed by Sir Alex that they've not made the starting line-up. But it's good news for Wes Brown, Gabriel Heinze and Darren Fletcher who are all in.

The squad return to the hotel dining area at noon for their pre-match meal and board the coach to Wembley around 12.45 p.m. On arrival at the stadium, the players head out to the pitch to sample the atmosphere. The turnstiles have been open since noon so there are already

The view from the coach as United arrive at the new Wembley.

plenty of fans inside the stadium which, on first viewing, is a hugely impressive creation.

The teams begin their warm-up at 2.10 p.m. for half an hour. Meanwhile, former BBC presenter Des Lynam is introducing a special parade of FA Cup legends from the last 50 years to mark today's historic occasion. United fans reserve the biggest cheers for former favourites including Lou Macari, Frank Stapleton, Denis Law, Mark Hughes and Peter Schmeichel. Sir Alex watches from the sidelines and greets a host of his ex-players as they head back down the centre tunnel.

Opera singers Lesley Garrett and Sarah Brightman enter 15 minutes before kick-off to perform the traditional cup final hymn "Abide With Me". Chief guest and president of the Football Association Prince William declares the new stadium officially open, before the FA Cup itself is given a grand entrance by veterans of the armed forces. The

Red Arrows perform a special fly-over just seconds before the teams, led by both managers, enter the stadium at around 2.50 p.m. United fan and tenor Russell Watson then leads the crowd in a rendition of the national anthem.

The game enters extra time after a goalless 90 minutes, which in truth has been a rather uneventful affair. Two minutes before the end of the first period, Giggs thinks he's scored when Petr Cech carries the ball over the line after saving the skipper's initial effort. In a bizarre incident, referee Steve Bennett gives neither a goal nor a foul against the Welshman, whose impact on the Chelsea stopper had pushed him over the goal line. The game looks to be heading towards spot-kicks, until Didier Drogba's winner four minutes from the end of the second period of extra time puts paid to United's double dream. It's heartbreaking for the Reds, but as Michael Carrick insists afterwards, the team have much

Trevor Lea, Tony Coton, Sir Alex, Mike Phelan and Carlos Queiroz check out the pitch.

The controversial moment: Ryan Giggs and Petr Cech collide; the ball crosses the line, but no foul or goal is given.

to be proud of at the end of an exhilarating season.

"To lose a final anyway is bad, but to lose it like we did after having a chance to win is devastating," he admits. "We are disappointed now because we really wanted to win this competition, but when we go away and look at the season we can be very happy with the way we have played and what we have achieved."

Welcome To KOREA

United are afforded
a special welcome
all over the world.

Part Six

SPECIAL OCCASIONS

"It's incredible to see the support we have across the world. It's hard to believe
people that live so far away from Manchester even know your name. It just shows
you how big this club is and the huge impact it has on a global scale."

DARREN FLETCHER

REDS GO GLOBAL

21

The arrivals hall at Incheon International airport in South Korea is buzzing with excitement and anticipation. A sea of red fills the floor as armed guards stand watch over more than 5,000 screaming locals. A similar scene is unfolding at a nearby hotel where the crowds are ten deep amid a cauldron of noise and commotion. You could be forgiven for thinking they are awaiting the arrival of a Hollywood superstar or a high-profile political dignitary. But this is the reality of a pre-season tour, because when Manchester United are in town it's big news.

The Far East is home to some 40 million Reds followers – over half of

Cristiano Ronaldo is given a hero's welcome in Tokyo in July 2007.

the club's worldwide fan-base. Their staunch and fanatical support for United is a sight to behold when witnessed first-hand, but it is the concentration of that backing which takes your breath away.

"I don't think we'll ever get used to the reception we get in Asia," admits Sir Alex Ferguson. "It's totally overwhelming and the intensity begins the moment you step off the plane. We usually train in front of more fans than those at your average Premiership fixture and the matches are always played before a very excited crowd. They even cheer our throw-ins! Taking the team to Asia is the least the fans deserve."

The arrival of Korean international Ji-sung Park in July 2005 and the acquisition of Chinese starlet Dong Fangzhuo have further enhanced the club's Far East profile now the locals have Asian players to cheer on at Old Trafford. The Reds' most recent visit to the world's largest conti-nent – in July 2007 – integrated new destinations in the form of Korea and Macau, as well as former haunts China and Japan. It was their sixth visit in 12 years and one of the biggest to date. United legend and club director Sir Bobby Charlton is a seasoned tour traveller both as a player and in his ambassadorial role with the Reds. Like his fellow knight, he too marvels at the overwhelming global support which United attract.

"Wherever I go in the world Manchester United are always the most popular team," he says. "I remember travelling out to China after we'd won the Treble in 1999 and I could barely make it out of the hotel lobby because there were so many fans camped outside. It's important that we try and see as many of our fans throughout the world as possible, because they can't all get to Old Trafford. We have to say thank you for their support."

Aside from the glitz and glamour that now surround the more high-profile tours such as those to Asia, South Africa and America, the trips represent a key component of the team's overall preparation programme for the new season.

"The level of football nowadays means pre-season is a crucial time and we always reiterate to the players how important it is to put the work in during that period," explains Sir Alex. "If they do that then they can gain their proper fitness, sharpness and mental awareness for the start of the season.

"The travel and conditions in places like Asia can make some trips

Opposite:
**A packed house
follows United's
every move on tour,
even in training.**

quite a daunting prospect for the players. But by the time we embark on the tours they have usually completed a great deal of fitness work at Carrington. The tour matches just add to their stamina and sharpness."

The advances in sports science over the last 20 years in areas such as fitness and nutrition has seen a complete overhaul of previously favoured training methods.

"The pre-season regime is completely different now to when I was a player," recalls Sir Alex. "During my career with Dunfermline, we used to go on eight-mile runs around local golf courses to get ourselves fit for the new season. That was the way it was back then.

"It wasn't until I took up coaching that I started thinking about pre-season training properly. When I went into management I curtailed all the punishing and gruelling distance running and brought in shorter exercises which focused on mobility and stretching."

Fitness coach Tony Strudwick is entrusted with coordinating and delivering the Reds' pre-season training programme. After consultations with Sir Alex and his coaching staff, including assistant boss Carlos Queiroz, first team coach Mike Phelan, goalkeeping coach Tony Coton and the club's medical and nutritional team, Tony Strudwick devises both individual and group plans for the players to follow.

"For the last fifteen days of their summer holiday the players follow a specific fitness programme which I have prepared for each of them," reveals Tony. "Given the fact they are returning to pre-season training on the back of a long period of rest, this ensures they are partly prepared and that their performance level is around the medium stage.

"I organise the training programme with the tour very much in mind. I look at the effects that the travelling will have on the players, as well as the humidity and heat if we're playing somewhere like the Far East. I also look at when there are opportunities for the players to rest."

There is particular focus on rest and relaxation during World Cup and European Championship years. Those players who make it through to the latter stages of the major championships are usually afforded a late return to Old Trafford even if it means they miss out on the pre-season tour.

"Players who come in to the start of a season after a big championship don't necessarily need much training or many games because

they have come from an environment where they've played concentrated football for over a month," explains Sir Alex who has the option to ready his returning international stars in post-tour domestic matches, which also form part of the pre-season programme. "Failure to get adequate rest during the summer can result in them becoming mentally tired later on in the season. Mental tiredness is the first thing that happens when players have had too much football."

For the players themselves, pre-season is one of the most challenging periods in the football calendar as they look to build up their fitness for the upcoming campaign.

"It's definitely the most difficult time of the year for a footballer but I do think it gets easier as you get older because your body becomes more accustomed to it," reasons club captain Gary Neville. "Between the ages of sixteen and twenty-two I found it really hard work; I can recall going home and collapsing on the sofa on a number of occasions!"

"There is certainly a lot of running involved and we train both in the morning and the afternoon," adds Darren Fletcher. "We don't see any footballs for a couple of weeks when we get back from our summer holiday because to begin with we spend most of our time working on our fitness."

Running is the order of the day during pre-season.

New signing Nani displays his trademark celebration after scoring his first goal for United against Shenzhen in July 2007.

Sir Alex and Nelson
Mandela come face
to face.

That lack of ball action is not something that sits well with Nemanja Vidic. "I'm not a fan of just running, I like running with the ball but not just running on its own!" he jokes. "I like everything that involves working with the ball, training without it is not something I enjoy."

"Pre-season is also one of the most important periods of the year," continues Neville. "It's when you get your base fitness for the whole season. If you miss it I always believe you're catching everyone else up throughout the campaign."

Despite the arduous sessions on the training pitch, pre-season isn't just about running; just like the tours aren't all about football. Factored into the team's hectic schedule are a number of community visits usually involving the club's global charity partner UNICEF. The United For UNICEF partnership, which is now part of the Manchester United Foundation set-up, was formed in 1999 and since then the Reds have helped raise over £2 million for a number of the charity's most high-profile projects including the Unite for Children, United against AIDS campaign.

On the 2006 tour of South Africa, Sir Alex Ferguson and his squad met former South African president Nelson Mandela at the offices of the Nelson Mandela Foundation in Johannesburg. The team wore

blue and red pin badges as a symbol of their support for UNICEF's HIV/AIDS campaign – a cause close to the heart of the work of the Foundation.

Sir Alex, a UNICEF ambassador, and a host of his players including fellow ambassadors Ryan Giggs and Ole Gunnar Solskjaer also paid a special visit to Tygerberg Children's Hospital in Cape Town to learn how HIV/AIDS and violence impact the lives of children within the Western Cape. On their arrival at the hospital the United party were shown a video detailing the suffering of children in the region, and indeed across South Africa. They then chatted with the youngsters, many of whom had suffered extreme physical abuse, rape and malnourishment, before taking part in an impromptu kick-about. The visit clearly had an effect on all the players, not least Ole Solskjaer.

"As a dad, I know how much I worry about my children and what I would do for them," he explains. "You look at the pictures and think 'how can people do such things?' It is easy to ignore it and pretend it doesn't happen, but someone has to stand up for these kids and show them that people care."

Future community visits, which will be coordinated through the

Paul Scholes meets youngsters during a community visit in South Africa in 2006.

Sir Bobby Charlton marvels at the skills of one young Red.

Manchester United Foundation, will continue to be an integral part of the pre-season tour programme as the club looks to lend its support across the globe.

"We recognise that the Manchester United name is a worldwide one and there is an international community that we can serve," says Communications Director Phil Townsend. "The pre-season tours will help us to do that and we'll be looking to involve ourselves in a range of overseas football and community projects. Our partnership with UNICEF has always been central to that."

Aside from community visits, a number of recreational activities, such as golf and snooker, as well as organised visits to some of the local attractions are also incorporated into the team's tour itinerary. Trips to the Forbidden City and Tiananmen Square during the team's stay in Beijing in 2005 were particular highlights, so too a night out at Yankee Stadium in New York in 2004 to watch the city's major league baseball team in action. A team excursion to a game reserve during the 2006 South Africa tour is one that will live long in the memory of two Reds – defender Patrice Evra and kit manager Albert Morgan.

"We were all taking photographs of the different animals and Albert decided to move a bit closer to one of the pens so he could get a better picture of this goat which was like a surrogate mother to an abandoned rhinoceros, but the edge of his glasses caught the wire of the cage and he suddenly started shaking before falling to the floor. I ran over to check he was okay but he didn't respond. He eventually came round but was still very dazed. He didn't realise that the wire was live and he'd suffered an electric shock."

"I honestly thought I'd been shot!" recalls Albert. "But when I turned around everyone was laughing hysterically behind me. I didn't get any sympathy at all. Patrice was laughing so much he could hardly stand up."

"I was crying with laughter by that point," continues Evra. "I laughed for about three weeks after that, every time I saw Alby! It's definitely the funniest moment I've experienced at the club."

Gary Neville's favourite tour anecdote involves Dwight Yorke's antics – or lack of them – on the training pitch during the team's tour of China and Australia in 1999.

"The lads were doing some stretching exercises on the ground at the

start of the session," he explains. "Everyone had been out the night before so were feeling a little delicate. The next thing we knew Yorkie had fallen asleep! The lads couldn't believe it. It's definitely one of the funniest things I've ever seen – I've never known anyone fall asleep during training!"

While the prime focus is centred on enhancing the players' fitness levels ahead of the start of the new campaign, pre-season tours are also a vital tool in helping to raise the club's commercial profile.

"Alex is the first to recognise that in order to get the players he wants on the pitch, we have to give some time over to the commercial side of the business and pre-season trips are a crucial part of our commercial set-up," explains United chief executive David Gill.

"The football season strikes me as getting longer and longer and the opportunity to organise these major tours is therefore limited to the years when there are no World Cup or European Championships.

"We have millions of fans throughout the world and only a small minority can make it to Old Trafford. So it's up to us to make sure we go and see them. We want our name out there and pre-season tours are therefore a key focus for us going forward."

Danny Simpson, Sir Alex, Wayne Rooney and Chris Eagles get to grips with a tiger cub in China.

Owen Hargreaves cradles a baby chimpanzee on tour.

United work closely with their commercial partners during their foreign tours.

The organisation of such trips, which are typically between ten days to two weeks long and are also attended by club officials and staff, as well as sponsor representatives, is primarily coordinated by marketing relationship director Luisa D'Aprano, who joined United in December 2005. With the help of a designated promoter based in the chosen destination, Luisa coordinates everything, including the travel (usually a private jet) and accommodation arrangements, the matches – which are broadcast live on the club's in-house television station MUTV – the media and commercial events and even the players' food requirements.

"About five months before the start of the tour, myself and Phil Morris, the operations manager from Travelcare Sports who are the club's official travel partner, fly out to wherever we're due to play to ensure all the planning and the logistics of the trip will fit against what the team need in terms of facilities at the hotels and the stadiums," explains Luisa.

"We compile a report on our return, which we then sit down and discuss with Sir Alex and his coaching staff so we can start planning the itinerary. The itinerary is probably the most complicated part of the process because there is only so much time available to do all the things we need to do.

"Our main focus is always on the football side. We want to ensure that the players have adequate time to train and rest before and after matches. We then look at how best we can include various press and commercial partner activities, as well as community visits, within the schedule. Once the preliminary itinerary has been drawn up I then make a return visit to our pre-season destination with the club secretary, Ken Ramsden, a few weeks before it is due to start, so we can finalise the details of the trip and also meet with the officials from the teams we'll be playing against to firm up the actual match details.

"Some years we'll be up against high-profile opposition like we were in 2003 and 2004 when we faced Juventus and Bayern Munich during the back-to-back tours of America. On other occasions we'll play local teams, usually in their home stadiums."

During the years in which the World Cup or European Championships fall, United will, as a rule, enter one-off pre-season tournaments which are organised by an independent body and are more low-key than the club's major tours. The non-championship years allow the Reds to coordinate trips across more time zones. Once a main destination has been selected for a major tour, the club must then decide which specific territories they will visit.

"That decision can be a complicated one, particularly when it comes to places like Asia," explains Luisa. "We look at various aspects, such as where our biggest fanbase is and where our partners' major operations are situated, so we can all benefit fully from the tour. We work very closely with our main commercial partners in order to try and identify which are the best markets to visit.

"We always work to a long-term plan and are constantly thinking ahead. There needs to be a balance in terms of where we visit, however. We're not able to visit Asia every year and likewise America isn't somewhere we can go each time either. It's all about trying to balance the football demands and the commercial demands on the tours. They need to benefit everybody."

Future jaunts across the Atlantic are, according to David Gill, something that the club are working on.

"The training facilities and stadiums are excellent in the States, but the American market is a challenging one and is consequently much more difficult to crack," he reasons. "We're biding our time at the moment and thinking about when and what we should do in America."

Another market the club spends time and money analysing is the counterfeit one. United's Trade Marks department, which has been running for over ten years, has seized nearly 300,000 fake items (including replica shirts, mobile phone accessories, scarves and even garden gnomes) worth over £5 million during the last six years in 32 countries. The creation and sale of fake merchandise is particularly rife in countries where United have a large following and labour is cheap; the club have seized £3.7 million worth of goods in China, Thailand and South Africa alone.

Tour time represents the department's busiest period. They begin their planning in February by making contact with lawyers and investigators in the appropriate countries in order to find out what enforcement options are open to them. This is followed by a pre-tour visit to allow the Trade Marks team, who work closely with Nike in the build-up to the trip, to train up foreign officials and assess the areas surrounding each stadium. In the weeks prior to the commencement of the tour they will up their raid activity if required and ensure it is well publicised. During the tour itself the department operates at open training sessions, and before and after matches, and seizes any counterfeit goods.

"The club are extremely committed to protecting their trade marks," insists a United official. "We work hard to send out the message that we won't tolerate the counterfeiting of any Manchester United products or trade marks, and we do whatever we can to assist those who actively enforce the legislation."

While pre-season tours are an ideal way for the club to make preparatory strides for the coming campaign both on and off the pitch, they remain a great opportunity for United fans worldwide to get a glimpse of the players they exalt from such an unfathomable distance.

"Our supporters around the world need to see us, and pre-season tours are the opportunity for that to happen," says Gary Neville. "In an ideal world we wouldn't spend fourteen hours on a plane flying to the other side of the world and then travel another three hours every few days around different countries. But we all realise that the club needs to commercially propel itself around the world – it always has done – and it's part and parcel of playing for United.

"America is a popular destination with the lads. The training facilities are excellent and because the game is not as high profile out there it means we can walk around virtually unnoticed. The intensity of the fans in Asia is very different. Over there we get thousands of people just coming to watch us train, such is the support for the club. Even walking out of the hotel can be hard work because there are always lots of fans waiting outside. Nevertheless, it's still mesmerising to see the level of support we have in that part of the world; they simply just love United."

Former MUTV chief commentator Steve Bower, who attended numerous pre-season tours during his time with the channel, never failed to be amazed by the team's Far East reception.

"I'll never forget the first time I went to Asia with the team, it was like landing with the Beatles or Michael Jackson," says Steve. "Fabien Barthez's blazer was literally ripped off his back by fans and there were girls just fainting at the sight of Ryan Giggs. The airport security guards were all United fans and when the team arrived they just stopped what they were doing and started trying to get autographs and pictures. It was just crazy."

"It's hard to believe people that live so far away from Manchester even know your name," admits Darren Fletcher. "It just shows you how big this club is and the huge impact it has on a global scale."

22 CROWNING GLORIES

Forget ending the season with a limp defeat. Forget missing the chance to relegate West Ham. Forget the teeming rain: 13 May 2007 was a day for remembrance. This was how it felt to be champions.

After a season-long sprint for the finishing line, United had beaten Chelsea to notch a 16th league title, and nothing was going to spoil the celebrations for a heaving Old Trafford crowd, and Sir Alex Ferguson's euphoric squad. A four-year sabbatical from Premiership domination had invigorated players and fans alike to rejoice in style now that United had returned to the pinnacle of English football.

The match itself, which saw Alan Curbishley's Hammers retain their

'We've got our trophy back!'

The coaching team celebrate winning the Premier League title in May 2007.

top-flight status despite the baying home contingent's demands to "send them down", was a footnote in United's season, nothing more. The hard work had been done over the preceding months, and finally everybody was going to see the Premiership trophy held aloft by the exhausted and exhilarated players.

Getting the silverware into the hands of the players is no mean feat, however. Weeks of planning, one bizarre dress rehearsal and a seven-minute window in which to set the stage made the whole project a tumultuous old affair.

United, the Premier League and Barclays were all involved in the presentation's preparation weeks before the Premiership had actually been won. Given that time frame and the tit-for-tat nature of the title race, it's of little surprise that the same officials who met with United also met with Chelsea, although ultimately in vain.

Club secretary Ken Ramsden and predecessor Ken Merrett led the planning process from United's viewpoint. Although the Premiership trophy's absence had been four long years, the pair's previous experience in planning such presentations proved vital.

"Without sounding arrogant, we've done this some times before so there's a confidence that the Premier League has in us that we can deliver what we say," says Ramsden. "We also have a confidence in them

A huge amount of planning goes into getting everything ready for the handing over of the trophy.

because we know they know what they're doing. There's a great deal of mutual trust around the whole thing, which does make the day and the job a lot easier.

"There's a standard procedure; there's a rig on the pitch, the fireworks and the confetti. We talked through that and looked at a timetable too, and had the tunnel measured. Because it is a big rig, they had to make sure that all the kit could pass through it. It would have had to be adapted if it hadn't fitted, but it did.

"One thing that did come up at the first meeting, when they showed us their drawing and model, was that behind the platform was a solid board with the sponsor's name on it. We pointed out that it would block the view of a lot of people in the North Stand. To be fair to the Premier League and Barclays, they took it on board and redesigned it to have a mesh effect behind. While that's maybe not perfect for those in the

North Stand, it did overcome it to a point. You have to be mindful of things like that and the fact that they accepted that concern and did something about it was reassuring."

There were 75,927 fans shoehorned into Old Trafford to witness the Reds' coronation, but the millions of worldwide television viewers meant that strict time constraints had to be implemented on the presentation process.

"The Premier League had allowed themselves a seven-minute window between the team leaving the pitch and starting the presentation," says Ramsden. "They've got to be mindful of the needs of television to get it included in the programme – and, of course, it's in our interests to have it on there too. Not that we're being driven by TV, but they've got a valuable role in the whole thing."

In order to ensure the presentation's smooth running on the day of the match, a trial run was pencilled in for the day before the game. Although events conspired to hamper, Ramsden and his counterparts managed to go through a full dress rehearsal at Old Trafford.

"When we were discussing this before everything had been settled, I was very mindful of the fact that, if the title race went to the wire, it could have been really embarrassing to be seen as arrogant or presumptuous if we were seen staging a presentation rehearsal," he says.

"Luckily it wasn't an issue, but we still had to work around the tours of the stadium and the museum. As such, the rehearsal took place on the Saturday night before the game. Unfortunately, it was a dreadful day and the weather was awful, and the groundsman took the decision that we couldn't do it on the pitch.

"The company managing the platform and rig had to make do with practising outside. It was all about carrying it a distance, making sure it looked right, putting it together and so on. On Saturday night a small number of us went onto the pitch to agree exactly where the rig would go, where the photo board would go – it's no good having it somewhere without working out where the photographers need it. It sounds obvious but it's important."

With the finer details of the event's logistics ironed out, one final stumbling block was laid before United by the Premier League.

"For the first time for us, they offered us the opportunity to decide

Darren Fletcher and
Ole Gunnar Solskjaer
enjoy a bite to eat
after the game.

Cristiano Ronaldo,
Patrice Evra and
Mikael Silvestre are
all smiles.

who would carry the trophy out on to the pitch," says Ramsden. "In some ways I wish they hadn't because it was a nightmare. Who can you choose? All sorts of people think they should do it, and so it was a bit of a poisoned chalice.

"One colleague suggested that we get some of the former players from the team of fifty years ago which was a phenomenal idea. We approached the seven survivors of that squad. Although one chap, Ian Greaves, couldn't make it because of a chronic back condition, he appreciated the invitation, and the other six were there.

"We were able to entertain them well. We got them round to the dressing room and they really felt part of it. I think the manager was delighted that they were involved. We believe it's that kind of thing which sets Manchester United apart. We've got a history, a tradition which some clubs haven't got and we want people to know that we recognise that. It was a marvellous opportunity for us to say to these former players that we recognise their place in history and they were glad of that. The only downside was that it poured down, which we couldn't control!"

And rain it did. So saturated were the players at the end of 90 minutes that Albert Morgan had to provide fresh, dry kit for each individual – even those who had played no part in the game, such as injured skipper Gary Neville.

While the stage was being hastily erected, the players too were

undergoing a swift change as they assembled in the Old Trafford tunnel. The simultaneous arrangement, together with West Ham's own celebrations, made for a frenetic air backstage. Again, though, Ramsden and company were prepared for such a situation.

"One of the other issues that crops up is the need for health and safety; a lot of rules have to be adhered to," he says. "So there was a lot of talk between our experts and others about things like fire certificates and fire extinguishers; a huge amount of work goes into making it a safe operation. We don't want to see a player get hit by a rocket just as he's lifting the trophy!

"There's a tremendous job going on in the tunnel which nobody sees, where everything is being manoeuvred while the players are trying to get off the pitch – in this case particularly the West Ham players. We were always mindful that it was a big day for them as well. They could

Wayne Rooney, Darren Fletcher, Wes Brown, John O'Shea and Nemanja Vidic proudly display the Premier League trophy they had worked so hard to bring back to Old Trafford.

217

have been relegated and we had to ensure that we remained respectful for their supporters. As it was, everyone was happy."

The day undoubtedly belonged to United, however, as they could finally rejoice at being atop the peak of English football after ten months of hard graft.

After all the players had filtered on to the pitch and received the winner's medals they had spent a lifetime craving, skipper Neville and Ryan Giggs – clinching a record-breaking ninth league title – lifted the Premiership trophy before their adoring fans.

Fanfare sounded, fireworks exploded and flames erupted all in time, just as planned. Old Trafford was awash with dramatic celebrations. Although the rain couldn't dampen anybody's spirits, it did manage to have a slight say in one of the presentation's neat little touches.

"The rain did have an effect on the confetti that was going out of the cannons in the background," confides Ramsden. "Unfortunately, it came out in big blobs rather than streamers, but we couldn't help that. At least everything else went well!"

The trophy was handed around the squad, before the players' families joined the party and the happy throng wandered around the pitch, parading the fruit of their labour. Fans hurled scarves and voiced their adoration, while players posed for pictures with their loved ones for personal mementoes. Meanwhile, those who set up the presentation prepared to dismantle it just as quickly. The clean-up operation began as soon as the last player had left the pitch, and within minutes there was no trace of their presence on the field.

The Premiership season is over. Now it's time for United to master-mind another ten months of hard work so that they may once again savour another fevered dose of pure, unbridled revelling, next May.